HOW *to* ATTRACT GOOD LUCK

D0881678

Jeremy P. Tarcher/Penguin

a member of Penguin Group (USA)

New York

HOW *to* ATTRACT GOOD LUCK

AND MAKE THE MOST OF IT
IN YOUR DAILY LIFE

A. H. Z. CARR

JEREMY P. TARCHER/PENGUIN
Published by the Penguin Group
Penguin Group (USA) LLC
375 Hudson Street
New York, New York 10014

USA · Canada · UK · Ireland · Australia
New Zealand · India · South Africa · China

penguin.com
A Penguin Random House Company

First published in 1952
First Tarcher/Penguin paperback edition 2014

Most Tarcher/Penguin books are available at special quantity
discounts for bulk purchase for sales promotions, premiums,
fund-raising, and educational needs. Special books or book excerpts
also can be created to fit specific needs. For details, write:
Special.Markets@us.penguingroup.com.

Library of Congress Cataloging-in-Publication Data

Carr, Albert H. Z.
How to attract good luck : and make the most of it in your daily life / A.H.Z. Carr.
p.   cm.—(Tarcher success classics)
ISBN 978-0-399-16736-2
1. Fortune.   2. Success.   I. Title.
BF1778.C37   2014   2013036541
158—dc23

PRINTED IN THE UNITED STATES OF AMERICA
1   3   5   7   9   10   8   6   4   2

for Toby and Peter

CONTENTS

Part Three
The Response to Chance

ACKNOWLEDGMENTS

Several hundred men and women, in many countries and walks of life, have been kind enough to contribute the true stories of good and bad luck which provided the raw materials for this book. While I cannot name them all here, I should like to take this opportunity to express my warm appreciation of their interest and co-operation. Especially, I am deeply grateful to some who have recently taken time from crowded lives to make material available—notably, Miss Malvina Thompson, the Right Honorable Winston Churchill, Senator Paul Douglas, and Messrs. Gerard B. Lambert, Nathan Milstein, Edward A. Wilson, and Francis Cammaerts.

In addition, I must speak with gratitude of the help and good counsel given me by my wife, Anne Kingsbury Carr, of the valuable contributions of thought made by Mr. David Horwich, Mr. Eben Given, and Mr. O. R. Johnson, and, above all, of the brilliant and penetrating editorial insights of Mr. Henry Morton Robinson and Mr. Jack Goodman.

A. H. Z. Carr
Truro, Mass.

HOW *to* ATTRACT GOOD LUCK

THE OPENING STATEMENT

"Anyone who does not know how to make the most of his luck has no right to complain if it passes him by."

CERVANTES

W ho has not sometimes wished that he were a more consistent favorite of that elusive element in life called luck, fortune, fate, or destiny? Under any name, luckiness, by general agreement, is a condition that men aspire to. With reason; it is luck that enables us to move unscathed among the hazards of the world, that touches our days with the color of adventure, that guides us down the long corridor of opportunity and quietly tells us which door to open. Every angler, whether he be fishing for trout, treasure, or tranquillity, must weigh his catch in luck's mysterious scale.

Yet, while with part of our minds we acknowledge luck

to be a great and valuable ally in life, at the same time, absurdly enough, the word is likely to evoke the image of a tinseled deity, crowned with a cheap alloy of superstition and fool's gold. The tribute paid to this deity is the poor coin most often found (along with a rabbit's foot) in the pocket of the petty gambler and the fortuneteller's victim. Repeatedly they make their futile offering, hoping against hope for a killing at the race track, the winning "policy" number, or top place in the office baseball pool. Feverishly they plunge in the market on the strength of a third-hand tip overheard in a barbershop. They quiver (if female) at the palmist's prediction that a tall, dark prince will ride up one of these days in a flamingo convertible. Caught in the toils of superstition, unable to rise above their immature notions of luck, they will never comprehend its deeper operation in human affairs unless luck itself lifts them into the light.

For luck, properly regarded, is not a painted and capricious trollop. Nor is it to be found in the dark-o'-the-moon vapor rising from a witch's cauldron. Luck, stemming as it does from the philosophic concept of chance, deserves to be classified among the prime factors in life—a force quite as constant in human affairs as reason or will. It is in this broad sense—viewing luck as a mighty, if unpredictable, influence in the lives of all men—that we undertake the present study.

Although luck cannot be measured by calipers or foot-rule, our hearts and minds alike attest its reality. The few who say, "There is no such thing as luck," are lost in a metaphysical quibble. Human awareness of luck—call it intuition if you will—extends from the bewilderment of primitive man to the highest speculative flights of theology and philosophy. In his vast summary of the divine plan, Thomas Aquinas allots a specific role to chance, the prime begetter of luck. In chance he saw God's instrument for testing the spirit of men. And modern science finds in the movement of stars and electrons dramatic proof that the random element of chance does indeed range the universe.

But proofs more immediate and persuasive pour in from a thousand human sources. Folklore, the colloquial wisdom of proverbs, and the common experience of mankind all testify to the existence of luck as a universal, not wholly understood, but never-to-be-discounted influence in our lives. We see these indications all around us. The father sending his son off to the wars with a grim "Good luck, son"; the Eskimo wife sewing a talisman in the coat of her seal-hunting husband; the actuary cushioning his hard tables with a plump pillow of "contingency" (the statistical name for luck); the wistful plea "Wish me luck" uttered by a friend setting forth on a risky journey; the roulette player grimly riding out a sequence of losses while he waits for the unpredictable turn of fortune's tide—all these give evidence of man's instinctive belief in "the magic hand of chance," which can by turns caress, stifle, or chastise. Significantly, it is from the old word "hap," meaning luck, that "happiness" is derived.

Men have always striven to find ways of improving their luck, and their efforts have generally centered around omens, portents, and black magic. The Roman augur, interpreting the flight of birds, has been succeeded in modern times by numerologists and clairvoyants attempting to peep into the future. Such puerile practices have degraded the whole subject of luck. At the very mention of the word, many intelligent people lift a skeptical eyebrow and pass on to a "more sensible" topic of conversation.

This skepticism is understandable. After all, what reasonable person would wish to link his fate with the haphazard pattern of tea leaves at the bottom of a gypsy's cup? Within the past generation, however, our view of luck has been lifted from the black-cat level to an infinitely higher and broader plane. Psychology has opened the gate to a new and rational approach to luck—an approach so strongly flanked by scientific concepts that serious men and women may now undertake the study of the luck-process without sacrifice of intellectual dignity or self-respect.

Armed with modern insights, those who seek will discover the true nature of luckiness. They will find that it is not a mere matter of poker winnings and the like but rather a *specific condition of mind*. The chief object of this book is to show how the lucky condition of mind can be attained—to describe the attitude toward life that makes for good fortune.

THE DIFFERENCE BETWEEN CHANCE AND LUCK

At the outset, we shall find it valuable to clarify in our minds the difference between "chance" and "luck"—words closely related, and often used interchangeably, yet actually not the same thing. Dictionaries define "chance" in such terms as "the unknown, or unidentified, cause of events not subject to calculation." To state the matter plainly, chance comprises the infinite number of unpredictable happenings, both great and trivial, that are constantly taking place in the world. A devastating volcanic eruption on a South Sea island, the aimless flight of a barn swallow from one rafter to another—these, along with the ripple on the water, the passage of a cloud, and all other events that we cannot specifically predict, fall within the category of chance.

Most of the chances we perceive in life we ignore, for they are without significance for us—remote, impersonal, external. But now and then a chance will touch the interests of an individual—and then it becomes very personal and significant indeed. *For as soon as human emotions are affected by a chance, it has been transformed into luck.*

An illustration may help to make clear this very important distinction. The wind blows a piece of paper across our path. We see it flutter in the distance, and we walk past, our minds on other matters. The paper has been set in motion by forces that we cannot control. It does not concern us. It has merely reached a given point simultaneously with ourselves, and the result is unpredictable chance—one of the myriad number of tiny, fortuitous events that befall everyone in the course of a day.

Suppose, however, that as the piece of paper flutters by, we follow it with our eyes, stop, and discover that it is money—a ten-dollar bill. At once the chance takes on a new character. It affects us, gives rise to an emotion, a warming glow of satisfaction. The impersonal has become personal. Chance has become luck!

Luck, then, is the effect of chance on our lives. But—and this is of vital importance—chance is not the only element in luck. Another factor is obviously involved—ourselves. For it is our *response* to chance that provides the counterpoint in the harmony of events that we call luck. Whether and how a chance affects us is largely determined by our own attitude and behavior. Not until we focus our attention on the piece of paper and stop to pick it up do we see luck in the chance of its passing.

Chance and response, between diem, provide the warp and woof of existence, and the pattern of every life. There we stand—receptive, intricate organisms animated by desires, thoughts, and behavior patterns—the sum total of our heredity and life-experience. The external chances of life play upon us—and as we respond to them, we shape our luck. Each individual among us responds in his own way. In a sense, every person is like a plant, which needs an occasional fall of rain in order to live and grow. When the rain—the favoring chance—comes, whatever happens thereafter depends upon the nature of the plant. One plant may flower magnificently and yield rich fruit, while another is almost barren. The important point is that *the luck of the plant, as of the person, depends ultimately upon the combination of external chance and inner responsiveness.*

As a concrete example: give one child a trumpet, and after a few desultory tootings he will never touch it again. But hand the trumpet to a young Harry James and a virtuoso career is set in motion. There is nothing intrinsically lucky about a trumpet. It is the chance impact of that instrument upon an eager, talented youth that creates, in the case of a James, the result we recognize as luck.

This, you say, is an extreme instance—and it is. Actually, of course, there are numerous less extreme possibilities of luck in this situation. Some youngsters would pick up the trumpet offered by chance, and by making a conscious response to its challenge might eventually find in the instrument a source of modest pleasure for themselves and others. A small degree of luck, but a gain, nevertheless, and it results from the combination of chance and response.

The same principle applies in the important luck of life—when chance aids us to the fulfillment of our deepest desires—in matters of health, love, prestige, living standards. This far-reaching, fundamental luck (as different from a race-track killing as genuine happiness is from an alcoholic spree) similarly comes not from chance alone or from us alone, but from both together. And we are far more likely to find this significant luck in our lives if we consciously lend ourselves to the fruitful interplay between external chance and inward response.

With that thought, we come to our central theme. It is this: *We can improve our luck by making ourselves readier for the chances of life as they come to us.* Shakespeare, a pioneer in the philosophy of luck, has written, "If it be not now, yet it will come. The readiness is all." The words have profound meaning. For the vigor of the effort that we make to be ready for luck may well be the deciding factor between a lucky and an unlucky life.

WHY SOME PEOPLE ARE UNLUCKY

Let us repeat: Good luck can be induced. It lies within our power to influence, not chance, certainly, but our relation to chance. And by that very fact, none of us can escape a measure of responsibility for his own luck.

How, then, explain the feeling of many persons that they have been unlucky through no fault of their own? Is this feeling justified, or is it self-deception?

In some cases, undoubtedly, people have cause to feel that they have been harshly treated by life. As we all know, many events, and notably misfortunes, strike us all of a heap, regardless of anything that we may have done or can do. The airplane crash or train wreck; the accidental death of a loved one; financial reverses caused by an unpredictable change in economic conditions; great catastrophes, such as fires, earthquakes, floods, epidemics, and wars—all these constitute what is sometimes called ready-made luck. To foresee such events or mitigate their impact on our lives is often beyond us; and so we must strive to accept them in accordance with our character and belief, either as a part of God's plan or as the unavoidable fall of chance.

But while ready-made bad luck does unquestionably account for the feeling of unluckiness that some people have, it is by no means the whole story. Or even half the story. There is another, far more common reason for the prevalence of bad luck in many lives. Psychologists have found that the unlucky person, more often than not, is the man whose behavior reflects profound insecurities of mind and spirit. *It is psychological insecurity (present, to some degree, in most of us) that normally prevents us from responding successfully to the chances of life.*

Underlying the bad luck that we bemoan, others can often discern better than ourselves the flaws of personality, faulty alignments with life, and infantile residues that prevent us from functioning as well-adjusted, luck-charged persons. But while most of the bad luck of life is directly traceable to the play of chance on psychological insecurity, it must be added that this is not necessarily an unchanging condition in any person. Because a man has failed in the past to respond adequately to the chances of his life, he is not thereby condemned forever to the limbo of the hopelessly unlucky. The whole potentiality of the future still lies within him. It is no mere figure of speech to say that every man carries with him an invisible *luck-potential,* which reflects the condition of his mind. And by means of conscious effort, such as this book outlines, it often lies within our power to increase our luck-potential to a surprising extent.

TURNING THE TIDE OF BAD LUCK

The victim of bad luck urgently needs to bear in mind that whatever the run of misfortune in his life, it does not signify that he has been singled out for destruction. With co-operation from him, his luck may turn at any time. For a long and unbroken sequence of ready-made bad luck is a rarity. The chances of life come to us, not on a dead level, but in a pulsating rhythm of gain and loss, and when men comfort each other with the reflection that it is darkest before the dawn, they have substantial evidence behind them. If we maintain a high level of readiness, sooner or later a favorable chance is almost bound to break through the unhappy drift of events and produce an unexpected burst of fulfillment.

Again and again life records that if a man goes on struggling, putting forth all his energy to hold his own against the onslaughts of mischance, the turn of the tide comes suddenly and carries him to safety. To quote again from Shakespeare (of whose majestic insights we shall avail ourselves often in this book), "In the reproof of chance lies the true proof of men." It is a primary lesson of life. As soon as we closely scrutinize actual cases in which bad luck has suddenly turned to good, we see the part played in the transformation by the qualities of the person.

As an example, consider the following incident. A woman of thirty-four, living a contented, quiet, middle-class life in Pittsburgh, Pennsylvania, was suddenly overwhelmed by four shocking blows of ready-made bad luck. Her husband was killed in an accident, leaving her with two small children. Shortly thereafter, one of her children, a girl, was burned on the face by hot bacon grease, and the mother, in great agony of mind, was told by the doctor that the child might be scarred for life. At the time she had a job in a small retail store, but soon afterward the store went out of business. Her husband had left her a small insurance policy but, it turned out, had failed to remit his last premium, and the company withheld payment of the insurance.

As the result of these misfortunes, the woman was close to desperation. Casting about for something to salvage, she determined to make one more effort to collect the insurance. Up to this point, she had been dealing only with subordinates at the insurance company; when she had tried to see the manager an officious receptionist had assured her that he was out. Now, arriving at the office, she found that the receptionist was away from her desk. The chance seemed providential. Walking without hesitation into the inner office, she found the manager alone in his room. A courteous greeting encouraged her, and with all the composure she could summon, she told him of her insurance problem. The manager sent for her file; when he had grasped the situation, he decided that the company had a moral, if not a legal, obligation to pay, and ruled accordingly.

But the luck resulting from this one chance had not yet fully revealed itself. The manager was himself unmarried; he and the young widow were strongly attracted to each other. He called on her, and in the course of the next few weeks the following developments occurred: (1) a doctor whom he recommended performed a skin operation on the child which removed all traces of the accident; (2) the manager, through a friend in one of the large department stores, obtained for the widow a job much better than the one she had held; (3) the manager asked her to marry him. Some months later they did marry, and the marriage proved happy and successful.

HOW GOOD LUCK CAN BE INCREASED

The story just related shows not only the mutability of fortune; it reveals further the process by which response intertwines with chance to produce luck. At the heart of this process lies *the vigorous assertion at the right moment of certain outstanding and positive characteristics.* In the case described, the characteristics are clearly alertness and courage. Had this woman not instantly grasped the chance presented to her by the absence of the receptionist and responded to it boldly, the ensuing good luck could never have developed.

But alertness and courage, while high on the list, are only two among a number of attributes which stand in a special and close relation to chance and which create a channel for the free flow of luck. Not all of these attributes, by any means, are the obvious virtues associated with wisdom and goodness. Observation tells us that it is not necessarily the "best person" who is the luckiest. We have all seen highly moral people, with pure and innocuous personalities, whose luck has nevertheless been bad. Even exceptional talent is no guarantee of good luck. Far from it. Talent has been known to walk the streets looking for the one ingredient that might have crystallized good luck out of fluid circumstance. On the other hand, many an individual who has been considered hopelessly inadequate, and who seemed doomed to failure and misery, has displayed quite late in life unexpected qualities that transformed his luck and thereby changed the entire structure and direction of his life.

Accumulated evidence shows that any constructive,

well-marked trait is a distinct asset in the pursuit of luck. Even such humble gifts as sobriety, thrift, and diligence strike useful notes in luck's larger harmony. Luck always tends to favor those who make maximum use of their equipment, whatever it may be. When a man not especially outstanding in mind or personality rises to extraordinary heights of satisfaction in life, it is usually because he has operated at the top level of his nature, has fully realized his potentialities.

The case of Harry S. Truman is a notable example. Universally regarded as a likable but not brilliant man, and even thought at one time to be a failure, he nevertheless was able to attain the highest distinctions and to achieve enormous gratifications both in his personal relationships and his public career. He has often been called lucky, and unmistakably he is. The adjective "lucky," when merited, means not only that a man has been helped by chance but, more important, that *he is the kind of man whom it is easy for chance to help.* Those who know Mr. Truman well agree that an essential element in his luck has been the effective use that he makes of his native equipment. Within his limitations, he has brought the best out of himself, and so has turned the chances of his life into almost miraculous luck.

As with President Truman, so with many of less renown. Analysis of hundreds of authentic case histories shows that whenever a man finds the way to the lucky life, the reason lies in his ability to make full use of his positive traits of character. If, at some point in a person's life, he becomes suddenly lucky, it is almost always because his lucky traits have been strengthened, his luck-potential has increased, and it has become easier for chance to help him.

Certain of these positive traits, as might be expected, are much more important than others in the luck-process. What they are, and how they can be developed, the pages to come will show. Not, of course, that we can expect to add cubits to our stature by taking thought. It is no use trying to develop a talent that we have not got, or to assume virtues that are foreign to our being. If luck-development demanded revolutionary changes in us, it would be a hopeless undertaking. Fortunately, it makes no such demand. On the contrary, the efforts that it asks from us are so modest that they are within reach of everyone. A strengthening of a single lucky characteristic that lies dormant within us or the disciplining of a single unlucky pattern of behavior has been known to lead to a sensational improvement in luck. Once we understand clearly what the goal is and how to go about reaching it, there is hardly one of us who cannot significantly increase his luck-potential. It is the purpose of this book to bring out the relationship of luck to various aspects of our nature and to indicate the ways in which lucky attributes can most readily be developed.*

These attributes fall into three major categories: qualities that attract lucky chances; qualities that help us recognize luck when it comes our way; and, finally, qualities that strengthen our response to potentially lucky situations.

Attraction—recognition—response. These are the three master-phases of the luck-process—all of equal importance, all interdependent. It is by better adjusting ourselves to this process that we make ourselves luckier. We shall draw on actual life-experience to see how each step in luck-development can be taken by anyone who approaches the task with an open mind and a genuine desire to improve his luck.

---

* There seems to be no existing word which precisely describes this subject. Perhaps it is permissible to coin one—"tychology," from the Greek *tyche*, meaning luck.

PART ONE

The Attraction *of* Favorable Chances

1

HOW ZEST EXPOSES US TO LUCK

"Come, bring me unto my chance."

SHAKESPEARE

Good luck, it has been remarked, usually strikes into the world of men with the suddenness of lightning. And the question which confronts us at the outset is: How can we attract this beneficent lightning into our own lives? Remembering that Benjamin Franklin caught nature's lightning when he sent a metal-laden kite soaring toward the clouds, we cannot do better than to borrow his principle: In order to attract luck, we must first expose ourselves to it.

This phrase, "exposure to good luck," is much more than a metaphor. It describes realistically the way in which we find most of our luck—a way so obvious that we often overlook it. Over many years hundreds of people have related the luckiest experiences of their lives to the author of this book. Many of the stories—in effect, case histories of luck—were the stuff of everyday experience, but others told of strange, almost unbelievable twists and turns of fortune. An analysis of the cases, however, showed that more than half of them had one thing in common: the lucky episode began for the person concerned at a time when he was exposed to others—*when someone else unexpectedly said something important to him.*

Often the thing said was in itself trivial; only by touching precisely the right conditions could it possibly have produced the luminous spark of luck. We see a simple illustration of the process in an example contributed by a Catskill farmer, who reports:

"A fellow from the city came up to the house last January and said his car was stuck in the snow. My son and I went out to give him a hand. We got to talking and he said he was manager of a new store in Kingston. Said he was going to open up a farm-equipment department. It just happened my son was looking for a job and this was right down his line. Worked out fine. Started as a salesman and now he is managing the department."

Commonplace? Perhaps. But unmistakably lucky! An everyday remark, uttered by chance, meshes with a person's interests—and the result is an important new fulfillment in life. We must, of course, recognize that the roots of such pieces of luck go far deeper than the incidents themselves. If the farmer and his son had not been the sort of men who are willing to go out in a snowstorm to help a stranger, the luck outside their door would have passed them by. But here we need only concentrate on the first important step in attracting luck: to recognize that *most of our good luck*—the beneficial effect of chance upon our lives—*comes to us through other people.*

Between ourselves and those who cross our path, chance spins an invisible thread of awareness, a "luck-line." (Since this word, luck-line, is much more convenient than "awareness of oneself in the mind of another," we·shall use it hereafter.) It is not too much to say that any new acquaintance to whom we throw out a luck-line represents a possible gain in our future luck and happiness. Not that we can tell which luck-lines will carry a live current of luck. Of the men and women to whom we talk, perhaps not one in ten, or one in a hundred, will make the unexpected remark that significantly touches us. But sooner or later, someone does—and that one remark can transform a life.

To expose ourselves to luck, then, means in essence to come into healthy human relationships with more people. The more luck-lines a person throws out, the more luck he is likely to find. Instinctively, each of us tends to form around him a kind of web of luck-lines, over which luck is transmitted from person to person. Lucky chances which touch any strand in the web may be felt at the center. Thus, the en-gaged girl, meeting an eligible new man, arranges to in-troduce him to her not-yet-engaged friend; and the man with a job, hearing of a good opening, tells his jobless neighbor about it.

THE STRANGER AS A SOURCE OF LUCK

Friends and family, as we shall see, play an important part in the lucky life. But—and this is a salient point—*a high proportion of lucky chances comes to us through strangers*, or from people we know only slightly. This is not really surprising when we stop to think about it. Most of our well-worn contacts, whether in domestic life, business, or social groups, soon lose their spark. We meet the same people, we say about the same things, we seldom hear a fresh thought or observation. After the first mutual curiosity has been satisfied, the ordinary mild friendship usually settles down into a conventional pattern, and thereafter is far less likely to produce the improbable, electric remark that makes for luck.

It is from dynamic bursts of common interest that good luck generally flows in human relations, and interest is usually at its peak and imagination at its nimblest in the earlier stages of acquaintance. You meet someone—the switch is thrown, a spark is kindled, a coincidence takes shape, or a chance piece of information passes—and there is the core of a lucky break. Many have learned from happy experience the meaning of Edwin Arlington Robinson's perceptive verses:

> There came along a man who looked at him
> With such an unexpected friendliness
> And talked with him in such a common way
> That life grew marvelously different.

"Unexpected friendliness." Here lies the secret of much of the luck of life. Age-old wisdom, embodied in folklore and legend, tells us to receive with open hands the stranger who comes to the door, for he may be the mysterious agent of good fortune. The Greek myth of Philemon and Baucis who, sharing their meager supper with two hungry strangers, found that they had been entertaining gods unawares, hints at a wonderful truth of life; and the ever-full pitcher of milk with which they were rewarded is the symbol of the nourishing luck that flows eternally from warmhearted relationships between men.

All of us are aware that not every stranger merits our interest, or can be trusted. We learn to guard against the aggressive bore, the malicious gossip, the ruthless peddler, and those dangerous men and women, human booby traps, who make it a business to prey on the innocent. But this does not mean that we need to cower in our shells like frightened turtles, while life passes us by. Nor can we afford to be "too busy" for new people—the excuse often given for a rejection of the world around us. The compelling fact is that no one who wants more luck in life can afford to let fear or indifference block him off from the potential luck of The Stranger.

ZEST—THE SHORT CUT TO LUCK

In enabling us to throw out luck-lines to strangers and old acquaintances alike, one quality beyond all others has almost magical power—the quality of zest. Bertrand Russell has called zest "the most universal and distinctive mark of happy men." We can say with equal truth that zest is the mark of most lucky men—a quality which, in the struggle of life, often overshadows and outweighs serious defects of character and limitations of mind.

To be zestful is to have within our minds a secret and inexhaustible fountain of youth. But zest, while it keeps the mind fresh and resilient, needs to be distinguished from the sheer exuberance and animal spirits of childhood. Zest is not a matter of boisterous movement and wild effervescence. It comes with the development of the mind—the word connotes appreciation, intelligent enjoyment.

Again, zest is very different from the lip-smacking greediness of gluttony. We have all seen the man who stuffs himself at table only to satisfy a gross appetite, without either savoring the food or understanding the cook's art. Gluttons of life similarly stuff themselves with experience merely out of greed, often neurotic greed, but without ever developing appreciation or understanding. Two types are especially common. One is the sexual glutton, the Don Juan, who restlessly seeks to possess numerous women without ever knowing the great joy of mutual love. Then there is the glutton of privilege, the man consumed by the need to outshine and outsmart and outpossess and overpower those around him—who is always demanding "the best," without ever being able to appreciate it or take real satisfaction in it since someone else always has a better best. Such men may be energetic in their gluttony, but they are far from zestful, and not likely to attract much good luck into their lives.

In a very real sense, true zest is a short cut to luck, for it quickly brings us within range of a far greater number of favorable chances than could otherwise reach us. To follow this short cut, we need to take an explorer's interest in the world we live in. The zestful person, while he may be occasionally angered or disquieted by events, loves life with all of its pains, absurdities, and follies. Far from wanting everyone else to be like himself, he finds pleasure in the rich diversity of mankind and in the endless variety of the human spirit. His curiosity on meeting new people is directed, not to learning what they may think of him or how much money they make or what they can do for him, but to the discovery of their personalities and their ways of life. In contrast to those who are quick to criticize and slow to praise, he is capable of hearty enthusiasm and appreciation of much that he sees and hears. The result is that people readily catch the luck-lines he throws out; and he has a far greater likelihood than the withdrawn or listless man of having luck come to him from others.

We need zest to counteract the feelings of anxiety which lurk in the shadows of every mind, taking a toll of luck. Anxiety lays waste our human relationships; the constant expectation of misfortune in our own lives is easily projected into the affairs of others, so that to friends and acquaintances we seem to be negative, pessimistic, even ill-tempered. Inevitably, the personality dominated by fear has difficulty in throwing out the fresh, healthy luck-lines upon which so much of our happiness depends. We need the cleansing agent of zest to sweep away the psychic cobwebs in which the imps of anxiety hide. Enabling us to adjust to our surroundings, bringing us into step with the world around us, zest is, in effect, an affirmation of life—a tacit declaration that its possessor finds it good to be alive, and wishes a full life for others as well as for himself.

To see in vivid detail how a zestful person unconsciously brings luck into his life, we need only take a specific example, such as an experience that befell the late and celebrated sports announcer, Graham McNamee. This was at a time when the radio industry had hardly been fledged, and McNamee was a young, unknown, and unhired singer. One day he received a call to jury duty at the Criminal Courts Building in New York City.

During a recess he observed a sign being put up on a building across the street. It had four meaningless letters on it—nothing more. Curious, he went over to the workmen who were hauling it into place, and learned that the sign comprised the code letters for a broadcasting station. He knew nothing about radio, but it occurred to him that just possibly they might have use for a singer. A moment later he was in the small office, speaking with the manager. The answer was a shake of the head. Accepting the refusal good-naturedly, McNamee took the occasion to ask some sensible questions about the mechanics of the business. At this display of genuine interest, the manager looked up. He was going into the control room, he said; would McNamee care to see what it looked like?

Zest, at this stage, had enabled McNamee to throw out

a fresh luck-line to a stranger; and the current of good luck was not long in flowing. After their tour of the station, the manager remarked thoughtfully that McNamee had a good speaking voice. They might need another announcer; perhaps he would care to make a voice test. In ten minutes, the test was made; in ten more, McNamee was hired; and one of the notable careers of radio was launched.

SEEDS OF LUCK

In McNamee's case, we have a quick completion of the luck-cycle: the zestful man—the stranger—the favorable chance—the stroke of luck. But often zest shows its influence on luck much more subtly, and over a much longer period of time. Its immediate reward may be merely a piece of information or a new idea—a seed of luck that only later flowers into reality.

The point comes through in a story from the youth of Winston Churchill, whom the world recognizes as one of the most zestful men of our time. The quality of zest showed itself in him even before he entered politics, when he was a young newspaper correspondent in the Boer War. Most of his journalistic colleagues were older and more experienced; when Churchill's extraordinary feeling for the dramatic and the bizarre began to bring him scoops, they looked upon him with cynical eyes, referring to him as "that lucky devil, Churchill." Lucky he was, beyond doubt; what they did not perceive was the extent to which his luck was attracted to him by his zestful readiness for any adventure.

On one occasion, a general gave Churchill a news story of great importance, causing heartache and whispers of favoritism among his colleagues of the press. Yet behind this success lay a typical, Churchillian display of zest. Days before he had ridden with other correspondents past a line of sullen Boer prisoners, when they saw one man who was knotting a bandage on his left arm with his right hand only, and doing it with great dexterity. On impulse, Churchill reined in his horse and asked the man where he had learned that trick. The wounded man, who spoke passable English, turned out to be a German, and a sleight-of-hand performer in music halls by profession. Interested, Churchill dismounted and walked along with the man, learning all that he could about him.

Later, he heard the British commander in the area express concern over the low spirits of his bored troops. Instantly Churchill had a suggestion: why not a sleight-of-hand performance by a talented professional? Challenged to produce the professional in that remote spot, he did, and the performance took place. It met with enthusiastic applause from the troops—and the general, to show his gratitude, gave Churchill an outstanding newsbreak.

An odd chance—a scrap of casual information—and the seed of luck had been planted, to burst suddenly into luck full-blooming when the right conditions arose. The running stream of zest carries to the fertile ground of the mind an endless number of such seeds. Men of the zestful breed, interested in every unusual manifestation of life, their minds open to the world around them, are walking reservoirs of potential good luck. The Churchills of the world, of course, are born seldom; but the way in which they invite luck by zestfully exposing themselves to new experience—by turning their minds away from themselves to the life around them—is a clue to the secret of their greatness.

It is a clue that, on our humbler plane, can well be allowed to guide us. Experiences recounted by many who have purposefully tried to take a greater interest in the world around them show that a relatively small effort in this direction can produce a very large and lucky result. The point is brought out in an experience related by a businessman living in a New York suburb, in these words:

"For years I have been taking the same commuters' train in the morning and talking to the same people. One night I had a quarrel with my wife and she said some things that shook me up. I don't mind telling you what they were. She said I was turning into a dull old man in middle age, and that I never took any interest in a new idea or a new person. She said I never said anything she hadn't heard Fulton Lewis say first. But what really hurt was her saying that I was turning into such a stuffed shirt that I would rather talk to a banker who bored me than a bum with an interesting story. She was right, and I knew it. The only people I talked to were those who agreed with me. The only newspaper I read was one that reflected my own opinions.

"I decided to do something about it. Next day on the train, instead of talking to my usual crowd, I picked out a fellow I had seen many times but never talked to. He was a dark, tough-looking character, and I had always figured him for some kind of racketeer. Not a bit of it. Turned out he was a public relations man who knew a lot about my business. He told me a good deal about himself, and right there, in that one-hour train trip, he sparked a couple of ideas that made a lot of sense. I asked him to call on me, and his stuff has been profitable for us from the start."

Moved by a conscious determination to expose himself to new acquaintances, this man found luck at his first attempt. Such instances, it is hardly necessary to add, are exceptional. The effort to throw out more luck-lines brings disappointments as well as pleasant surprises; not every new acquaintance is rewarding. But immediate luck is only a by-product of the development of zest. Our real aim is the state of mind that prepares us for a lucky lifetime.

The mere fact that we make the effort to be zestful carries far-reaching and lucky implications for our future.

BREAKING THROUGH SHYNESS TO LUCK

For no one is zest more important than for the young man or woman of marriageable age, who needs the help of chance to find the rich fulfillments of love. The unanticipated meeting with a stranger of the opposite sex that leads to mutual love represents a high peak in the range of luck—a peak which we are far more likely to reach if we bring zest to the search. Zestful exposure to new acquaintances plays a far greater part in the success of love and marriage than many realize or admit. When people are so limited in human contacts that they desperately plunge into matrimony with the nearest person, and without regard to mutual suitability, their chances of finding happiness in each other are not bright.

The zestless, unsociable person is usually one whose shyness has cut him off from most of the chances of love and of life. It is this unhappy trait, shyness, that prevents millions of otherwise promising human beings from throwing out a normal number of luck-lines. Almost everyone, of course, has moments of shyness; that is normal and does little harm to luck. The habitually shy person, however, is bound always by invisible cords of social timidity which prevent him from reaching out zestfully for the chances of life even while he yearns for them.

It need not be so. Shy people can often slip their cords of fear and develop zest more readily than they realize. The starting point lies in awareness of the real nature of the affliction. Many a shy person tells himself that his self-effacement reflects modesty, and is, by implication, really a virtue. He is generally wrong. Psychology reveals that the really shy person is likely to be *not so much modest as vain*. The vanity, to be sure, shows itself in an inverted form—in withdrawal, instead of aggressiveness. But the fact remains that the shy man generally avoids fresh human contacts because he is unwilling to run the risk of possible dislike or disapproval by others. On the one hand, he usually has an exaggerated idea of his own importance, thinks that people are much more concerned with him than they really are. On the other hand, he has an awful suspicion that no one else will recognize the qualities that he secretly believes himself to possess. Rather than expose himself to criticism and reveal imperfections, he prefers to remain aloof from life, taking refuge in silence, pretended hauteur, or absence from social gatherings. As a result, lucky chances which might otherwise come to him through human agencies strike the wall of his shyness and expire on the spot.

As soon as the shy person recognizes the real import of

shyness, as soon as he stops trying to excuse it to himself, he prepares for the effort to develop zest and throw out more luck-lines. Probably the most feasible approach open to him is through deliberate practice in meeting and talking to people. Painful as this process may be, especially at the beginning, it is often highly effective. Why is shyness so much more prevalent among the young than among their elders? The answer is that age normally brings with it a higher degree of realism. Older people tend to lose their self-consciousness in social contacts, because experience teaches them that if they do not have distorted ideas about themselves, the world will generally accept them as they are. As the shy person learns by repeated experiment to reveal himself simply and frankly to acquaintances, the heartquake of shyness begins to be outweighed by newfound zest in living. And when zest enters into life, luck is usually close behind.

In throwing out new luck-lines without falling victim to self-consciousness, shy people are helped by one relatively simple expedient—*keeping their thoughts away from their own problems.* By talking about things outside themselves, they can often manage to forget their inner qualms, to interest others, and to invite luck. A revealing story illustrating this point comes from a young woman whose shyness threatened at one point to blight her life. Although old friends with whom she was herself found much sweetness in her, she had grown up so self-conscious that she found it impossible to relax in the presence of strangers. At parties she was stiff and miserable, and she seldom made a new friend. Unmarried at the age of twenty-eight, acutely conscious that she was making a failure of her life, she became increasingly morbid, depressed, and withdrawn.

Then, one evening, an odd chance touched this sad life. The young woman had been invited to a party but had made up her mind not to go. Riding on a bus from her office to her home, she took the only empty seat. Directly in front of her were two noisy men, who, she soon realized, were drunk. Presently one of the men began to tell a long, rambling joke, and his attempts to remember it, together with his friend's interruptions, amused the girl so much that, before she recollected herself, the bus had taken her miles out of her way. The home to which she had been invited, she realized, was nearby; prodded in this way by chance, she decided to go to the party after all.

Ordinarily, after greeting her hostess, she would have retired to a corner with a fixed, unhappy smile and an untouched drink. But now the stimulation of laughter was still in her. Spontaneously she said, "I must tell you what I just heard," and proceeded to do so, with mimicry that surprised herself. Others in the group stopped talking to listen and joined in the appreciative laughter. As she described the experience subsequently, she said: "All at once I saw, for the first time, that it was easy to entertain people, and to make them like you. There I was, doing it. I had the most wonderful feeling of exaltation."

This young woman's lucky discovery that she could release her personality in the presence of strangers by forgetting herself and talking about external things seen and heard was for her like a rebirth into a better world. To learn to externalize one's conversation is to take an important step toward the conquest of social timidity. And there are still other, equally effective methods by which shy people can bring more zest and more luck into their lives. In fact, these methods are worth the attention of all of us, whether we be shy or forthcoming. They can be summed up in the phrases, "Try something new," "Find a center of interest," and "Expand your ideas."

THE LUCK OF SOMETHING NEW

It is a matter of common experience that the mere learning or doing of something a little off the beaten track can contribute surprisingly to zestfulness. Even a fresh approach to a stale pursuit will often bring, by way of zest, an unexpected accession of pleasure in life. Consider, for example, the case of a young housewife, a person of charm and intelligence, but whose dislike for cooking was for a long while a sore spot in her marriage. Not that she admitted her aversion. Instead, she rationalized it into a principle, saying that she thought people paid too much attention to food and that she believed in plain, simple fare. That was an understatement. The unimaginative, monotonous, and insipid meals she threw together, generally out of cans, took a heavy toll of her husband's patience, and of her own good nature. But she would make no compromise with the kitchen; when a friend gave her a book of unusual and interesting recipes for beginners in cooking, she tossed it aside unopened.

Late one afternoon an unexpected visit from her husband's boss—a man with a hearty appetite and a love of good food—created a crisis for her. His good will was essential to their hopes of the future; to inflict one of her customary dinners on him was unthinkable; an extraordinary effort was clearly required. Groping for help, she turned to the neglected cookbook. The first recipe she read—a casserole—sounded good, seemed to be within her modest capabilities. Prayerfully she tried it, and nervously brought the result into the dining room. Its success amazed her; husband and guest gave her praise such as she had never had at mealtime.

The effect of this small culinary achievement was to

change her entire attitude toward the challenge of the pots and pans. For the first time she wanted to meet that challenge, for now she sensed the possibilities of satisfaction in cooking. A few months of study and experimentation put her on the road to becoming a first-rate cook; but far more important, her relations with her husband improved, she found more zest in every aspect of domestic life, and she came to regard this episode as a happy turning point in her marriage.

Many another, like this young woman, has found that a more zestful and luckier life was the reward of a little attention to something new. For the human mind, however ingenious and imaginative, requires constant stimulation from the external world in order to keep its sap and spring. The symbolism of the old custom by which the bride wears something new at her wedding is entirely valid, for it recognizes the lucky chain that links novelty to zest and zest to happiness. By giving something of ourselves, a little mental energy, whether to aspects of familiar living that we have neglected or to new surroundings and new people, we develop zest. We feel more zest when we listen to a man who tells us something that we do not know, even if he challenges our opinions, than we do at the banal words of agreement. We usually feel more zest when we try our hands at a new sport or game than we do repeating a stale pattern of activity.

HOW A CENTER OF
INTEREST LEADS TO LUCK

The more concretely we think about the ways in which zestful feelings are generated in us, the easier we perceive the development of zest to be. Experimentation of almost any kind makes for zest. And so does the discovery of a successful avocation or hobby—a well-defined core of activity that fills the gaps in life and provides stimulating material for thought and conversation. Whenever a person's energy overflows his business, domestic, and social routines, a well-chosen hobby can go far to channel his vitality into more zestful and luckier living.

Two specific cases show how the alliance between hobbies, zest, and luck operates. One can be quickly summarized: it is that of a bored, rather sullen young man who received a camera as a birthday gift, became interested in amateur photography, found it exciting, joined a camera club, made new friends, and in a year underwent a highly desirable personality change. The other story is even more revealing of the power of a center of interest in bringing us within range of luck. A childless married woman, thirty years of age, is the chief figure. She envied the young mothers she knew, with their consuming interest in their children. Her husband's work required him to be away for long periods of time, and her emotional life was "running down," as she put it. She felt out of things; nothing interested her, nothing held her attention. When she and her husband, recognizing her need for a child, approached an adoption agency, they learned that thousands of applications were ahead of theirs and that it might be years before a child was available for them.

One day a stray kitten miaowed at this young woman's feet. On impulse, she picked it up and gave it food. Soon the little animal ingratiated itself into her affections, and she decided to keep it. When her husband objected, she defended the kitten's place in the household with more animation than she had displayed in a long while. Not only did the kitten provide an outlet for frustrated maternal affection, but more, it became a source of zest. The young woman began to read about the care of cats, and initial interest rapidly grew into a systematic hobby. Other cat owners, finding her well-informed, asked her for advice. The kitten's antics provided ever-fresh amusement, and added substantially to her pleasure in life.

Impulse into hobby—hobby into source of zest—such had been the sequence to this point. The lucky link in the chain was not long in forming. A little girl living nearby was fascinated by the kitten, and asked permission to come to play with it. Later, the child's mother called, to express her appreciation. The ensuing chat brought out the fact that the mother was a member of an organization for aiding European orphans—and that it might be possible to arrange an adoption from this quarter in a relatively short period of time. Within a year a little French boy came to live with the young woman and her husband, and the adoption proved a complete success. All the satisfactions of her life multiplied from this point. The kitten had partially filled a gap in her life with a zest-producing core of interest; and zest, leading to luck, had closed the gap completely.

LUCK FROM FRESH IDEAS

While sparkle and tang can be brought into pale and jaded lives by the effort to develop a hobby or to experience something new or to meet more people without shyness, the pursuit of zest need not end there. Still another approach is open to us. We move toward zest and luck merely by giving our minds more sustenance to feed on. And our main instrument for this purpose is the written word. A piece of writing can often give us a feeling of zestfulness, much as if the writer had spoken to us face to face. The words may be in a letter or printed in a newspaper, magazine, or book or spoken by an actor or reporter in a movie, television show, or radio broadcast. Their importance to our luck lies not in their form but in their freshness—their ability to stimulate and vitalize our minds. By expanding our range of thought and conversation, fresh ideas make us fuller, richer personalities, more interesting, both to ourselves and to the people whom we meet.

Frequently, the things we read with zest are coupled directly with strokes of luck. Even a sentence or two, found by chance, has been known to set off a train of lucky events, like firecrackers, ending in a Fourth of July explosion of good fortune. For example, early in this century two men, Joseph V. Horn and Frank Hardart, owned a modest Philadelphia restaurant. Horn had often daydreamed about mechanical dispensers for food which would make it possible to operate without waiters—but it was only a daydream; no such device existed, so far as he knew. One day he picked up a business magazine and his eye fell by chance on a brief item. It spoke skeptically of a new foreign invention of the slot-machine type which could be used in purveying food. That was all Horn needed. He disregarded the skepticism—investigated—and a few years later he and Hardart owned the large, famous, and profitable chain of Automat restaurants in the East. As in a conjuror's trick, the wand of chance (embodied in a few written words by an unknown journalist) touched a responsive vessel—and out popped the rabbit of luck.

The luck of the written word and the fresh idea also shows itself in far more profound, if less tangible, ways. In one instance, a marriage was saved when chance brought a Boston woman to a summer theater in the Connecticut countryside, and she saw a revival of a play of many years ago, *Craig's Wife*. The many who have seen this famous play know that it tells the story of a woman who, under the guise of self-sacrifice, ruthlessly sacrifices her family to her own feelings of insecurity. Watching the story unfold, the lady from Boston saw herself as in a mirror, and realized the extent to which she was responsible for domestic troubles that she had been blaming on others. Shocked and frightened, but also awakened and stimulated as she had never been before, she went home, had a long and honest talk with her husband, and was able to re-establish their marriage on a far firmer footing.

To expect a direct return of good luck for every effort to expand our ideas would, of course, be absurd. The fact remains, however, that the person who wants to add to his zest and luck in life does well to expose himself to many mediums of information and entertainment, from the newspaper to the theater, from television to friendly correspondence. Not that all of these mediums have the same luck-value. It is safe to say that grownups who habitually read comic books (and there are a surprising number of these children in adult bodies) expand their ideas a good deal less than if they devoted the same amount of time to, say, newspapers or magazines. Zest is not to be cheaply bought by slothful minds. It is only when we make an effort of attention, and give something of ourselves to the reading or the hearing, that we add significantly to our luck-potential.

That is why books have a special place in luck-development *The effort of attention needed to read a book, and especially a book with serious content, impresses it strongly on the memory, so that its ideas can be readily evoked by passing chance and brought into lucky use.* A surprisingly large number of lucky experiences center on books discovered by chance. For example, United States Senator Paul Douglas of Illinois, as a young man, still groping for a point of view toward life, happened to pick up, in the University of Chicago library, a book called *The Journal of John Woolman.* Woolman was an eighteenth-century Quaker of passionate conviction, which he was able to communicate to Douglas at a distance of two centuries. To another, the book might have meant little, but it was as if Douglas's personality had been waiting for precisely this enriching chance in order to unfold. It brought him new understanding, new zest, new energy, and went far to shape his subsequent brilliant career.

Every well-read person has had the experience of being strengthened at crucial moments by things read in books. To read to excess, to become bookish at the expense of firsthand experience of life would be obvious folly, but most people err on the other side; *they weaken their luck-potential by not reading enough*. It is an unlucky fact for many families that whereas they spend hundreds of dollars a year on television and radio sets, on motion pictures and fantasy magazines, they would consider it an extravagance to spend ten dollars a year for a few good books! Such people fail to comprehend that while the effortless, push-button, page-flipping forms of entertainment demand little from us in the way of attention, they also give us little in the way of reward; they plant few seeds of luck in our minds.

The busiest and most successful people, it may be noted, are the ones who read most. That is only to be expected. The person who is interested in many things and will make an effort to find out about them forges a strong link in the chain that leads to luck and achievement. "I have no time to read," more often than not, is merely an excuse for the unpalatable fact of a lazy mind.

There are many roads to zest. Whether we take the approach of more productive reading or a hobby or new experiences or the broadening of our human contacts, the effort cannot fail to expose us to a greater number of favorable chances. With every added increment of knowledge or experience, our luck-potential is enhanced, our probability of finding luck increased.

HOW GENEROSITY INVITES LUCK

*"Do you know what it is,
as you pass, to be loved by strangers?"*

WALT WHITMAN

While the quality of zest brings us within range of luck, it does not, of course, guarantee that luck will reach us. Many a person circulates widely, assiduously exposing himself to luck, without finding much of it in his life. The reason is clear enough. Not only the number but the *kind* of luck-lines that we throw out—the kind of awareness of ourselves that we establish in the minds of others—is of major importance in determining our power to attract luck. The luck-lines of some unfortunate people seem for the most part to be negatively charged. They may get off to a good start in their contacts with others; their energy and enthusiasm promise well; and then—something happens. Instead of good luck, they suddenly find that they have been tempting misfortune.

A typical case of this kind helps to disclose the source of the trouble. In this instance, a well-connected young man, on whose education thousands of dollars had been spent, volubly expressed bewilderment over his difficulty in keeping a job. "Don't get the idea it was anything I did," he told an older friend who had tried to help him. "I got along fine, every one of these places. But the breaks have been against me. This last place, they had to cut down on personnel in my department, and naturally, they wanted to keep the men who had been there longest."

But the head of the last company that had let him go, an advertising agency, privately had another version. "The boy means well," he said. "A friendly type, in fact he's a great glad-hander. His trouble is that he talks too much, and always about himself. The people in his department said unanimously that he was a nuisance. The last straw came when he struck up a conversation with a stranger in the reception room and told him he was writing copy for the W. account. That was one of those half-truths—we let him try his hand at some copy, but we had no intention of using it. Unfortunately, the stranger was Mr. W. himself. He was sore clear through when he came into my office and said, 'Since when are you letting unbaked cubs work on my account?' It took me an hour to calm him down. The boy's uncle is a good friend of mine, and I didn't want to tell him what I really thought, so I let him out as gently as I could."

Here was an instance of misfortune flowing from a normal, healthy, zestful impulse to make new acquaintances. The unfortunate youth evidently had no trouble in establishing contact with others, but within a few minutes his relationships took on a negative character. Let us come directly to the central fact. The young man was unlucky because *an unchecked ego was in his way.* He wanted so much to be admired and appreciated that he unconsciously exposed himself to heavy blows from chance.

WHY THE UNCHECKED EGO THREATENS LUCK

Probably no human frailty is more likely to bring bad luck into a life than an exaggerated need for appreciation. This unhappy state of mind, which usually grows out of a rooted feeling of insecurity, drives its victim to advertise his importance and demand that the busy world pay attention to him. Inevitably, he cuts off favorable chances which might otherwise emanate from others. Because the egoist tends to be inattentive when others are talking, he causes acquaintances to take a passive attitude in conversation and to withhold information and ideas that might have luck-value for him. Even more serious, he inclines to brag, boast, and show off, if sometimes in subtle and indirect ways. People who thus massage their egos in public, demanding recognition for their virtues and talents, generally are unaware to how great an extent they cause others to withdraw inwardly from them.

But even men who consciously realize the unfortunate consequences of ego-indulgence are sometimes unable to control themselves when they meet strangers, so compelling is their need for appreciation. One sees this triumph of the ego over common sense and good manners in the case of an Army colonel who asked for bad luck, and got it. He was a relatively young man, and no fool; and he had just been given his first command post, a small camp in a rural area. Civilians living near the camp hospitably invited him to their homes, and meeting some of them for the first time, after a few drinks, he felt impelled to talk about himself. In his actual relations with his men he was apparently fair-minded, but now he struck an almost Prussian pose—he was going to let these strangers know what a strong personality he was. "I believe in taking a firm line with my men," he said, and then went on to describe the severe punishments he had meted out for offenses which, as he described them, seemed trivial.

His hostess protested. "I understand the morale problem up here has been pretty bad," she said, "and I should think that kind of discipline would make it worse."

"They have to learn the hard way," said the colonel sternly, and went on talking.

A month later this officer was bewildered by orders from Washington relieving him of his command and transferring him to a far less attractive post a thousand miles away. Luck had spoken—the woman whom he had rebuffed had a brother high on the Army staff, and she mentioned the incident to him. Possibly other pressures already had been brought to bear against the unlucky colonel, and it took only this added evidence to weight the scales decisively against him. The fact was that by translating a sense of insecurity into an aggressive demand for appreciation, he charged his luck-lines negatively. Only a small chance was then needed to produce a disastrous stroke of bad luck for him.

GENEROSITY—THE LODESTONE OF LUCK

The chronic egoist is always a candidate for misfortune. Weakness—and unchecked egoism is a reflection of spiritual weakness—attracts bad luck with painful regularity. It is hardly surprising, then, to find that the strong characteristic opposite to egoism, generosity of spirit, consistently acts as a magnet for favorable chances.

To observe in practice how the power of generosity operates in the luck-process, it will repay us to consider in some detail an incident that befell the great violinist Nathan Milstein, when he was a very young man. At that time, several years before the outbreak of World War II, Milstein was touring middle Europe. One day he was on a Czechoslovakian train, en route to Budapest, where he was to play an important concert. At the Hungarian border the train stopped, and a surly Hungarian officer swaggered through, looking at the passports of the travelers. When he came to Milstein's passport, he barked out that there was an inaccuracy—the passport specified that Milstein was to enter Hungary by way of Pressburg, and here he was on a train from Prague.

Milstein explained that he had come from Prague because he had played a concert there. The technicality was obviously the result of some clerk's error, and not important, but the officer wanted to show that he was important. Ignoring protests from the other passengers, he ordered the youthful violinist off the train and told him to return to Prague. There was no recourse, and on the platform Milstein ruefully watched his train vanish in the distance, and pondered his problem. No other train to Budapest would run on that line until next day—yet somehow he had to reach Budapest in time for his concert.

When a voice addressed him by name, he turned to see

another Hungarian officer—this time young and amiable. A music lover, he had recognized the young virtuoso from photographs in the newspapers. Speaking in French, he told Milstein that he deeply sympathized; the other officer was an old crank, disliked by everyone, but nothing could be done. As for automobiles—unfortunately, there was none to be hired in that little provincial town.

Accepting the situation philosophically, Milstein invited the friendly officer to dine with him, and carrying suitcases and Stradivarius violin, they went to a little restaurant nearby, where Milstein was enthusiastically received by the proprietor. Soon the eyes of all the other diners were on the violinist, and they were whispering about his plight. From murmurs around him, it was obvious that everyone longed to hear him play. Good-humoredly, Milstein volunteered, remarking that since he could not play his concert in Budapest, he would at least play part of it then and there. Standing in the small provincial *café,* he played with no less feeling and care than he would have put into a performance for the gala Budapest audience. When he finished, there was wild enthusiasm, and men and women gathered around to thank him and to shake his hand.

Among those who spoke to him was a stranger, unknown to the townspeople. This man said that he was shocked to think that Milstein might miss his concert. An idea had just occurred to him. Nearby was a hunting lodge belonging to Count Esterhazy, one of Hungary's most powerful nobles, and a noted patron of music. The count was away—but his steward was at the lodge, and he, the stranger, knew the steward. Even if they did not have an available car there, if Milstein were to drive all night behind two fast horses. . . .

Within an hour the stranger, the officer, and Milstein were at the lodge. The count's steward heard the story, and instantly fell in with the plan. Why, his master the count was even then in Budapest, where he expected to attend the concert! Unthinkable that Milstein should be prevented from appearing because of the caprice of some jack-in-office! The steward called for a carriage and a driver—and with warm farewells, Milstein headed for Budapest and a spectacular success.

Few men can so easily create good will in large numbers of people as a superlative musician. But this story rewards analysis, for it strongly suggests a means by which any man can strengthen his invitation to luck. The essential facts are these: Milstein showed generosity of spirit when he volunteered to play, in order to give pleasure to strangers, and in spite of his own worries. Others in the room were already aware of him. Normally their awareness would have thinned away in a short time, but it was sustained and intensified by his generous action. One of them, the stranger, the agent of Milstein's good luck, had chance information of value to the violinist. Superficial awareness of Milstein's problem did not bring it to his consciousness. *But with his attention sharply focused on the violinist, the crucial fact came to him, and he felt impelled to pass it along to Milstein.*

An element of final mystery in the ways of fortune may always elude mankind, but we do not have to be mystics to accept the thought that generosity attracts good luck. Psychology gives us a strong, practical reason for this association. Bespeaking a fundamental good will in the human heart, generosity tends to evoke a similar feeling in the hearts of beholders. *Your warm-spirited actions intensify and sustain awareness of you in the minds of others. And the concentrated favorable attention of others increases the probability that they will remember a fact or conceive an idea beneficial to your interests.*

Thus it is that, in a very large proportion of lucky episodes, an act of uncalculated generosity figures in the chain of events.

YOU CANNOT DRIVE BARGAINS WITH LUCK

Uncalculated generosity. The adjective should be noted. Displays of good will for the purpose of obtaining reciprocal favors, or making people grateful, are far less likely to produce favorable chances. Few people really enjoy being grateful, and the emotion of gratitude has often been known to turn into ill-feeling after a short period. Calculated acts of giving are usually felt by the beneficiaries to be nothing more than a cold investment, made in order to get a return, and their minds are consequently far less likely to produce from the depths of the unconscious those luck-charged morsels of association on which so much may depend. No doubt cold generosity is better than no generosity at all; it will usually attract more favorable chances than outright selfishness; but the luck-lines of the man who strikes a generous pose in order to get something out of it are likely to need frequent repair.

The unmistakable truth is that you cannot drive bargains with luck. To expect a return for generosity is self-defeating. Material gifts, used to serve practical ends or to compensate for personality defects, have no more relation to generosity than pointing a gun at a man has to courage. Even what is commonly regarded as charity is often a long way from generosity, and still further from luck. True charity is one of the noble virtues, but all have seen many an instance in which charity was an act of condescension, performed to inflate the ego of the giver—and yet other cases in which it represented nothing but a desire to evade taxes. There is nothing in such false giving to attract good fortune; in the words of Lowell, "The gift without the giver is bare."

A distinction should also be drawn between genuine generosity and the compulsive and almost frantic displays of giving which some neurotic persons make. Not infrequently people who sincerely believe themselves generous, and would give the shirts off their backs, are only self-deceivers. It is not generosity that moves them so much as anxiety to be loved. Unconsciously they try to cement their friends to them with the material semblance of generosity. It does not occur to them that, as evidence of a warm heart, the conspicuous gift is often much less significant than suppression of the unkind remark that rises to one's lips—the effort to understand another's problem in his terms—or encouragement given when it matters. And since, in the luck-process, it is only the inner spirit of generosity that counts, those who give solely in material terms have done little to invite luck into their lives.

THE RESERVOIR OF LUCK

The luck which comes to us as a result of true generosity, we must observe, seldom takes the form of spectacular, immediate blessings out of the blue. While Milstein's story shows that this does indeed happen occasionally, yet, as we all know, a man may do a hundred generous things without having luck come his way. Certainly, luck is no mere caboose hitched to the train of generosity. The real reward of the generous is invisible and secret. It lies partly in their own psychological health and partly in the hearts of others—in the reservoir of good will fed by the springs of admiration and affection.

The generous person creates an unsuspected potential of good luck that needs only a touch from chance to burst all at once into happy reality. Sometimes such luck may take years to reveal itself. Here, for example, is the case of a schoolteacher in a small Massachusetts community, a woman whose warm humanity had endeared her to two generations of pupils. No one realized, when she retired, that she lacked adequate funds to assure her a dignified old age, for she had always kept her problems to herself. Reluctantly she decided to go away to live with a relative—and then luck entered, through the back door.

A chance miscalculation of her bank balance caused this fine woman to overdraw her small checking account for the first time in her life, compelling her to visit the president of the little bank to ask his indulgence. In the course of the conversation, he found it necessary to inquire about her finances, and shook his head over what he heard. She went away desolated—and her distress increased when she was asked to appear at a special meeting of the Board of Selectmen of the town. These tight-lipped gentlemen had assembled a group of leading citizens, and when she arrived they arose in a body and cheered. She heard then that the Selectmen had broken every precedent by voting town money to create an honorary post for her, carrying with it a home and an income as long as she lived; the town could not afford to lose her, they said.

This is not an isolated instance. In fact, the generous and idealistic spirit often attracts good luck through others even where there has been no close association. Thus, we have Gertrude Samuels, a *New York Times* correspondent, visiting Japan in 1951 and learning accidentally of an act of generosity performed by an American Army sergeant. Single-handed, tirelessly, and without publicity, this man had raised funds among his comrades, a dollar at a time, to rebuild a ruined orphanage for Japanese children; and Miss Samuels was so stirred that she wrote an article that gave Sergeant Hugh O'Reilly national prominence, although she had never laid eyes on him.

Even our enemies may serve as agents of luck when the generous spirit is called into play—as in the case of a political boss, a piratical old grafter, who repeatedly and publicly denounced a prominent reform leader in his city. On the surface, certainly, there was nothing in this relationship to suggest that either man could be the agent of good luck for the other. But the reform leader was a man of great and warm spirit; and as so often is the case, this was enough to throw a span of luck across the gulf between them. When the reformer, a poor man, fell seriously ill, a letter from a hospital arrived, stating that anonymous funds had been provided to assure a needed operation for him. Only years later did he accidentally discover that the money had come from his old antagonist, who had gone to great trouble to keep his identity hidden. The reason? A not uncommon one. There was something about the reformer's idealism that secretly attracted the other, in spite of their political enmity.

Humanitarian idealism, one of the loftiest expressions of the generous spirit, always has great power in attracting luck. The classic case is that of George Washington, who by the nobility of his nature threw out countless luck-lines to men he had never seen. Here was a man allied by birth and position to the Tories of his time, and yet he took an extreme risk of life and property to lead a revolution that was democratic in spirit. All over the world he was loved and revered by other idealistic men, and one of them, the French dramatist Beaumarchais, with the help of chance, produced an almost miraculous stroke of luck for Washington. By pledging his own fortune, and taking great personal risks, Beaumarchais was able to provide French aid for the American revolution long before the King of France was willing to act; and this aid was of high value in preserving the morale and fighting strength of Washington's army.

GENEROSITY, FRIENDSHIP, AND LOVE

Although few of us feel the call to idealistic self-sacrifice, nevertheless, we too have means of storing up lucky good will in the hearts of many others—means that all of us can afford, whatever our financial limitations. We can attract luck not only by yielding more frequently to our generous impulses toward strangers, when occasion offers, but also by the conscious and consistent practice of true friendship toward those we know well.

The word "true" needs emphasis. All of us want friends, but many people confuse the outward forms of friendship with the inner feelings. Like the salesman in Arthur Miller's grim play, *Death of a Salesman*, they take false comfort in the thought that they have many friends, when, in reality, they have only acquaintances who, like themselves, go through the ritual of the beaming smile, the hearty handclasp, the slap on the back, the solicitous inquiry. These may be agreeable customs, but they have little to do with friendship, and still less with luck. In luck-development we need to keep well in mind this seemingly obvious, yet easily neglected thought: *In order to have real friends, a man must be capable of being one.*

The key to genuine friendship—to the generous spirit that strengthens our invitation to luck—is not in the superficial attitudes of friendliness, but in the practice of good feeling, in the habit of well-wishing. There are specific ways by which we can encourage this habit in ourselves, simple and familiar ways. We can, for example, try a little harder to understand the problems of a friend, and to give him such assistance as we may without looking for a return. When a friend is troubled, we can suppress remarks that only add to his pain without helping him. When our friends are made happy by good fortune, we can fight down our envy and try to enter into their gladness. We can be less chary of merited praise, less intent on proving our superiority, less competitive, less assertive. To begin needs only a slight effort of will, a determination that this day we shall convey by word or action that we wish well to some worthy person of whom we have been neglectful or envious. No more than a telephone call or a letter may be required of us. The important point, for our purpose here, is that *every act of true friendship is proof of a rising luck-potential within us.* Such actions are like oil, lubricating the psychological mechanism of generosity which so many allow to rust unused within them. And it is when this mechanism begins to turn freely, when people sense within us the truly friendly, well-wishing, generous spirit, that they feel good will toward us, and a positive charge begins to course through our luck-lines.

The will to generosity is equally productive of good luck in the intensely emotional relationship of love. Many people, especially the young, seem to feel that successful mating depends primarily on finding the right person, and neglect the fact that it is equally important to *be* the right person. Although most people fall in love a few times in their lives, only the chance that brings two "right persons" together can open the way to the great luckiness of reciprocal love. That is why those who approach their relations with the opposite sex in a spirit of selfish calculation unconsciously weaken their invitation to luck. The cynic is never the right person. If he is male, he regards love as a mere sentimental cover for the sexual impulse; if female, as bait in a man-trap. Both play the parts of cheats in life—always an unlucky role.

Such people seldom stop to reflect that they pay a high, indeed a terrible, price for the pleasure of exploiting others. This love-rejecting cynicism works like a poison in the personality, producing the insecurity that tempts misfortune. Psychologists know that we need the love of others to maintain a lucky state of mind. The deep, instinctive craving for security which is in all of us cannot be fully satisfied except when we have the consciousness of being loved, first by parents, then by friends, then by persons of the opposite sex, finally by our children. By destroying love where he finds it, the cynic undermines the foundations of his own psychological security, and so turns his back on luck.

Sometimes, to be sure, the man who is unable to liberate his affections from the prison of the ego, and who never permits himself a wholehearted love-relationship, may, if he is vital and interesting, enjoy a certain temporary popularity with women. Sooner or later, however, his inability to deal with them as personalities, rather than as mere instruments of sensual pleasure, is bound to weaken his hold on happiness. This is equally true, of course, of the ruthless female rake who, scorning men in her heart, translates the love-'em-and-leave-'em philosophy into terms of power and hard cash. She is seldom as lucky as she thinks; she takes the easy tricks, but loses the game. Poets and novelists have long told us that when chance brings two lovers together, they can experience the highest fulfillments only when both are capable of generosity; and it is a lesson that life quickly verifies for all who can see.

GENEROSITY AND THE LUCK OF THE HOME

Generosity attracts luck by creating not only potentially lucky personalities but also luck-charged situations. This is especially noticeable in the play of chance upon problems of marriage and domestic life, which put unusual pressure on husband and wife. If, in spite of strain, they manage to maintain a generous attitude toward each other, they can often shape a situation in which it is easy for chance to come to their rescue.

A striking illustration is the story of a young couple who one day received the painful news that the husband's father had died suddenly of a heart attack. The problem then arose: what of his mother, who had been left penniless and alone? This couple had one small child and were living in a small city apartment. The husband could not afford to support his mother elsewhere. He put the problem before his wife, and she agreed that they ought to ask the mother to live with them.

The mother, a woman of considerable force of personality, tried, like her daughter-in-law, to make the best of the arrangement, but the problems of adjustment in that little home began to prove too much for them. Within a few weeks serious tension began to develop, until the wife had a sense of being trapped. She found herself thinking constantly of escape—even of leaving her husband, whom she loved. Finally, she decided that she must take some action.

Her first step was a long, honest talk with her husband. His understanding and sympathy with her problem gave her comfort, and his answer was unhesitating: he would find some other place for his mother to live, and she would have to get some kind of job. With her earnings and such sums as he could spare, she might be able to get along.

To the wife, however, it was plain that the thought of his mother, a woman in her fifties, working at some menial job was intolerably distressing to him. Now another solution occurred to her. Her need was to remove herself physically from the older woman as much as possible. She had worked before in her life; she would get a paid job and relegate the task of keeping house to the mother. Since she was not willing to leave her infant son to his grandmother's discipline, she would use her earnings to keep the child at a day nursery.

Husband and wife agreed that they ought at least to try this expedient; and although the thought that she was in effect being forced out of her house in the daytime was bitter to them both, it was so arranged. A few days later the wife found work as a saleswoman in a department store, leaving the mother in control of the home.

The situation, while improved, was far from satisfactory. The wife especially resented her daily separation from her child. Half of her earnings went to pay for his care. Nevertheless, over a period of months she was able to save several hundred dollars.

Then she had an inspiration, such as could only come to a woman of generous spirit and strong imagination. After a talk with her husband, they bought a television set, which he presented to his mother and which was installed in her bedroom. The mother was so captivated by the private entertainment, which she could command at will, that she left her son and his wife far more to themselves in the evenings, and her presence in the house was much less felt.

At this stage, the gain from their mutual generosity was largely psychological. They had enabled the husband to live up to his feeling of obligation to his mother, and at the same time, their common front added to their mutual respect and love. Potentially, this was a lucky situation; only a favoring chance was needed. It came as suddenly as such chances usually do. They had been dimly aware that his mother had made some friends in the apartment house, a few of whom had come in from time to time to view television shows. One night she simply announced that she was going to marry one of their neighbors, an elderly widower with an adequate income, whom they had never even met. It appeared that he had been spending afternoons at the apartment, as a television guest, and that they had found much in common. Within a week the marriage took place, and the problem was solved. So happy a solution, it is apparent, could not have materialized if, in meeting the original problem, this couple had been less generous in their attitude toward each other.

The conscious effort of each partner in a marriage to prevent unnecessary pain for the other is one important way in which generosity reveals itself and raises their luck-potential. Whenever a difficult problem is met with mutual consideration and understanding—whenever an angry or caustic remark is suppressed until a merited criticism can be made without a violent shock to the ego—an increment of good fortune is deposited, as it were, to the account of the home. But there is also another, more subtle, but no less important, expression of marital generosity—in terms of time and attention. This form of generosity is essential to the health of a marriage; it prevents feelings of frustration and hostility from eating away the family luck.

In no aspect of domestic life is generosity of time and attention more significant to luck than in the relations of parents and children. Many a parent who shows normal regard for the physical well-being of his children is yet so ungenerous in this larger sense as to build up a dangerously unlucky potential in the home. A startling case, exemplifying this point, was described by a close relative of the family concerned in these words:

"I cannot understand it. My brother is a good man— careful, industrious, sober, thrifty. His wife is a good woman and a good mother. She does everything in the world for her children, works herself to the bone. But they have had one terrible piece of bad luck after another. Their oldest boy played around with a fifteen-year-old girl and got her pregnant, and they had to buy off the girl's family. Then their daughter was caught cheating in school, and they had to beg the principal not to expel her. It was a terrible humiliation. Then yesterday the other boy, aged six, was playing with a pair of scissors and accidentally stuck one of the blades into the eye of his little baby sister, and she may lose the sight of that eye. It's just heartbreaking, the way misfortune dogs those people."

Heartbreaking—unlucky—yes. But the luck-pattern of this unhappy family revealed some significant character-istics. All the father's copybook virtues did not prevent him from being uninterested in his children, and ungen-erous of his time and attention. Preoccupied by his own concerns, he "did not want to be bothered" when he was at home—an understandable but fundamentally unlucky attitude. Inevitably, over a period of years, this attitude, becoming ingrained, began to produce large indirect consequences in the family. One of them was that the mother's attempts to compensate for the father's indifference led her to indulge the children beyond wise limits. The potential of bad luck thus created was like a bomb, waiting for chance to light the fuse.

Why had the eldest boy, still in his teens, got into so much trouble? No one had ever talked to him candidly about his sexual problems and responsibilities, and at the same time he lacked self-restraint. When chance brought him together with a naïve girl, bad luck was the natural consequence.

Why did the daughter cheat? A few questions revealed that she was so eager to win attention and approval from her father that she readily violated her self-respect to obtain high grades in school, when chance afforded an opportunity.

Why did the little boy play with scissors? While this is not an uncommon circumstance, yet it was found here that the youngster habitually chose such dangerous toys, knowing that no penalty was attached to anything he did. Chance and his little sister had done the rest.

Although other factors no doubt contributed to this situation, there can be little doubt that its main root lay in the father's attitude. He had failed in that final generosity which, transcending the material, leads men to give freely of themselves, and to make those near to them feel wanted and warm. Inevitably, he allowed unlucky psychic forces to build up around him—which, when chance touched them, promptly yielded up their charge of misfortune.

Whether in our relations with those we love, those we like, or those we casually meet, we cannot escape this plain fact: Selfishness invites bad luck, while *our warm-spirited behavior tends to pull lucky chances toward us.*

PART TWO

The Recognition of Chances

1

TURNING POINTS

"Whatever fate befalls you, do not give way to great rejoicing, or great lamentation . . . All things are full of change, and your fortunes may turn at any moment."

SCHOPENHAUER

A Chicago businessman, in discussing the subject of luck, remarked that in the early part of this century, someone had offered to sell him, for a few thousand dollars, a substantial interest in a small business called the Ford Motor Company, and that he had turned the offer down without even looking into it.

"If I had only had sense enough to investigate," he said mournfully, "I would have put up the money and made millions. But so many rickety little companies were looking for capital then. How could I tell that particular one was special?"

It is a pertinent question, not only in matters of investment, but in every aspect of luck. What can we do to prevent the favorable chances of life from slipping by unnoticed? The recognition of luck is just as important in the luck-process as its attraction through zest and generosity.

Hermits excepted, our lives are studded with chance situations that call for decisions. We are asked to meet someone or to advise a friend or to go to a party or to do some extra work or to take a holiday off the beaten track. We are tempted to quit our job or to tell a difficult person to go to the devil or to express an unpopular opinion in a group. Any such chance, and thousands of others like them, may prove to be a turning point in our fortunes or our psychological development. Any one of them can enrich the future with warming friendships, new interests, wider culture, happy memories, the thrill of achievement, enhanced self-respect, or greater earnings and prestige. Any one of them, in other words, may bring us good luck. But which? Few need to be told that many a chance, like a wormy apple, is rosy outside and rotten within. There are chances, too, which can bring luck to one person, yet offer no hope of luck to another. The need is to recognize among the myriad chances of life those which hold promise for the particular psychological package which is oneself.

Successful recognition of luck-in-the-making brings into play a wide range of qualities of personality and mind.

To the extent that we possess and develop these qualities, we are in an advantageous position to distinguish between favorable and unfavorable chances. Five such qualities are especially marked in case studies of luck. Alertness is one of them; the others are self-knowledge, judgment, self-respect, and intuition. It is essential now to survey the part played by these attributes in luck—and to determine how they can be most readily strengthened.

CATCHING THE RHYTHM OF CHANCE

The physiological basis of alertness, we know, is a tension of nerves and muscles prior to an event. A good example of this tension can be seen in a dozing cat disturbed by a noise. The cat does not know what caused the noise, but instantly a change takes place in its appearance: its eyes open, its ears twitch, it shifts its posture slightly so as to be ready for swift movement. That is to say, it becomes alert. So, too, with human beings. The expectation of an event sends through our brains an exciting message to our neural and muscular systems, inducing a state of tension. When the event occurs, the tension is released. While it lasts, we are alert.

Our problem, if we are to keep alert for the turning points that are so important in the lucky life, is really to encourage a state of tension in ourselves at the right times. In effect, we must decide when to expect a favorable chance.

Here you may cry, "Absurd! Chance, by definition, is unpredictable. How, then, can we hope to know what to watch for at any moment of our chance-filled lives?" It is a fair question. To live in a perpetual state of alertness would be clearly intolerable, even if the normal ebb and flow of energy permitted it. Our need is for alertness at the moments when it is most likely to be rewarded.

To anticipate those moments is not at all impossible. *Chance, which produces the effects in our lives that we call luck, has its own ways of behaving.* It is comprehension of those ways that helps us to be alert for turning points in the sequence of life's chances. True, we cannot tell what any one chance will bring. But the more we know about the ways of chance, the greater the likelihood that we will recognize favorable chances in time to transmute them into luck. Especially we need to become aware of two marked tendencies in the fall of chance: *rhythm* and *interconnection*. Understanding of these characteristics can carry us a considerable distance in luck-development.

Although everyone is familiar with the rhythms of nature, all too often their importance to human luck and happiness is overlooked. We sense these rhythms at every turn of life, from the dance floor to the grainfield, from the doctor's stethoscope to the astronomer's telescope—in music, in the stars, in the living organism itself. Who has not sometimes felt suddenly at one with the beat of nature, and found himself thereby more energetic, more alive? It is then that we work harder, dance better, love more deeply, understand more fully, have a wonderful aware-ness of identification with the universe. Everyone who has ever lived in the country knows the sense of well-being, almost a state of grace, that descends on the man who watches and loves the alternation of the seasons, the slow cycle of growth and harvest, the journeys of the birds, the interplay of nature's thousand rhythms.

Farmer and city dweller alike become happy when they feel themselves in step with nature. And it is lucky to move with nature's rhythm, not to resist it; lucky to make love when we are young, lucky to sleep when the mind signals us for rest, lucky to work at the job that comes naturally, and at times when energy brims. Especially we see the importance to our luck of these large, natural rhythms in the recurrent fertility of women, who in their whole lives have only a few hundred days on which they may conceive children. Should none of these days coin-cide with a woman's sexual fulfillments, she loses the chance of motherhood, and remains with her deepest instinctive urge unsatisfied. Her happiness depends heavily on the conjunction of a period of fertility with the chances of intercourse.

Beyond these familiar cyclic rhythms in us and around us is another—more elusive, frequently offbeat, its tempo never twice the same, but definitely there—the rhythm of external chance, as it plays upon our lives. We sense it everywhere—in games, in human affairs, in the weather. Catch the rhythm, and luck may be ours; miss it, and we miss a chance at happiness. Our problem is to try, so far as we may, to bring our internal cycle of energy, our undertakings, and our work into beat with chance.

An example suggests something of the nature of chance's rhythm. Tex Rickard, the fabulous fight promoter of the last generation, was famous for his luck where weather was concerned. Hardly ever did rain interfere with the great open-air boxing matches that he staged in the seasonable months of the year. Once he confided to a friend the principle on which he selected his lucky dates, months in advance. It is certainly not a scientific principle, and yet no scientist could do better. Rickard would study the weather records for years past, and pick a date on which in previous years there had been *more* than a normal amount of rain. He knew that the probability that rain would fall on any one day was the same as for any other day in the month. But he also felt that after a run of rain on a certain date, there was a good chance that the weather-luck of that day would turn. And, as his record showed, chance lived up to his expectations.

Always, where chance operates unimpeded, we find a broadly rhythmic alternation of rain and shine, heads and tails, good and bad. It is not, we must repeat, an even, unbroken rhythm. We certainly cannot predict precisely how long any one run of similar chances will last. But we can learn to expect the alternation of runs of chance; moreover, we can learn to expect it more at certain times than at others. *The runs of chance in life are normally short.* After similar chances have appeared in succession several times, we have every reason to expect a change. Take a familiar example—a coin tossed in the air. Toss it 4,096 times, and we find (in all probability) only six runs of eight or more successive heads or tails. The great majority of the tosses will be either "singles" or runs of two or three—short runs. So, too, in roulette. The longest run of any one color recorded at the Monte Carlo tables is twenty-eight successive "reds," and the probability is that such a run will occur only once in 268,435,456 spins of the wheel.

The implication? We cannot miss it. Watch the roulette players after red has come up five times in succession. See how they shift their bets to black. True, they may still lose—roulette players should expect to lose—since red may come up a sixth time, and a seventh. But *the knowledge that an early alternation is due calls for expectancy and alertness.*

THE OFFSETTING CHANCE

How can we take advantage of the alternating rhythm of chance to improve our luck? Chiefly by bearing in mind one simple fact: *A single favoring chance, recognized by an alert person, often has the power to offset a run of bad luck.* The game of poker offers an analogy. A good poker player will sometimes go through an evening of bad hands, losing consistently. Then at last he will receive a good hand. Preserving a casual calm, he bets with insight into the psychology of the other players, and builds the pot up to large dimensions; and although this may be the only pot that he wins during the evening, it can offset all his losses. To accomplish this, of course, he has to maintain his morale—to avoid depression, timidity, nervousness. Only in this way can he be alert to the full possibilities of luck in the cards that appear in his hand.

So, too, throughout life. If, after a run of unfavorable chances, we can remember to turn our minds from our own anxiety to the external situation in which we find ourselves, we make it easy for the offsetting chance to come through to us. When men find something that has seemed irretrievably lost, when they are luckily rescued at the moment of disaster, it is usually because they have kept alert for any chance that might help them. A dramatic example comes from the noted yachtsman, Gerard B. Lambert. He recalls that just before a race, his yacht "Yankee," lying at anchor off Newport, Rhode Island, was struck by lightning. Damage was slight; only the compass needed readjustment, and the boat was taken out to sea for this purpose. All appeared to be well. But overnight, as Lambert learned later, the rearrangement of the magnetic forces in the hull left the compass four points wrong. No one knew it; there was no opportunity to test the compass again before the race, the course of which ran along the New England coast.

In Lambert's words: "The race began in a dense fog, so thick that you could barely make out the starting line. The boats were soon separated and out of sight of each other. We were sailing, of course, by compass. In about half an hour, Ray Hunt, one of my afterguard, exclaimed, 'I don't like the looks of those lobster pots!' I was at the wheel and was too busy to have seen them. I agreed it was a bad sign. We should have been well off shore, away from pots. Only a few seconds after that we heard a hail from the port side forward. We were doing about ten knots on a very close reach, and the sea was so still we could hear almost anything. The voice floated out of the fog, just two words,

'Come about!' There was no warning of where we were, no long conversation, just 'Come about!' We never saw whoever it was.

"Even before I yelled my order, I started spinning the wheel to starboard. I knew now where we were, for I am familiar with that coast. We were headed straight for solid rocks that rose directly from the sea—one hundred and sixty tons at ten knots headed straight for them, and nothing around for miles but impenetrable fog.

"Luck? Why was a lone man in a small boat, probably a fisherman, at that spot on a lonely coast, and why did he have the God-given sense to yell 'Come about!' instead of trying to talk to us? I don't know, but it probably saved some lives."

The instructive point of this story is the speed of Lambert's reaction when he heard the enigmatic warning out of the fog. The accident to the compass and the presence of the lobster pots had alerted him to the possibility of further trouble. He did not permit anxiety to dominate his thoughts. All of his senses were focused on the external situation. As a result, he was alert to recognize the offsetting chance and to make the swift response required when it appeared.

Only by striving to maintain a high level of alertness at times when disaster threatens can we take full advantage of life's rapid shifts. To be spiritually weakened by misfortune is to invite further misfortune. Whenever there has been a run of unfavorable chances in a life, the victim needs more than ever to muster his energies and power of attention and to keep alert. It is astonishing how often and how swiftly bad luck can change to good—when alert behavior gives it encouragement to change.

THE PYRAMID OF LUCK

As the rhythm of chance often points to the turning points of life, so also does the characteristic that we have called *interconnection*. From time to time two or more interlocking chances in close succession touch almost every life. And it is at the points where this happens that luck reveals its power most dramatically. At such times, by alertness, we can often "pyramid" our luck, using the luck of the first chance as a steppingstone to the greater luck of the others. A significant illustration of this process came out of wartime Washington, when it was most crowded. A Midwestern advertising man, Mr. B., had gone to the capital to work for a government war agency, leaving his wife and children behind until he should find a suitable place to live. For weeks he searched for a house or apartment without success. Meanwhile he lived in a dingy hotel room, until the hotel management, which made it a rule to accommodate only transients, warned him that he must move. He felt angry and depressed; and at the same time he worried over the condition of the business he had left in order to fulfill his patriotic duty.

That night, caught by a sudden rainstorm, he took refuge in a doorway, where he was joined by an Army officer. While they were waiting for the rain to ease, a conversation got under way between them, and presently Mr. B. mentioned his housing problem.

"Maybe you're in luck," said the officer. "I've just had word that I'm being shipped out, and I'll have to get rid of my apartment in a hurry. Like to see it?"

Two days later Mr. B. moved into a comfortable apartment and sent for his family. But before they arrived, a second chance interlocked with the first. He was standing in a line in a government cafeteria, when the man in front of him dropped some cutlery from his loaded tray. Mr. B. helped him pick it up, they exchanged smiles, and found themselves sharing the same table. The stranger turned out to be a businessman just arrived in Washington to negotiate a government contract. Presently he remarked that he expected to spend the night on a park bench for lack of a hotel room. Responding to his genial and uncomplaining attitude, Mr. B. said that he would be glad to offer a bed at his new-found apartment. This invitation, gratefully accepted, laid the groundwork of a warm friendship. A few months later, a third interlocking chance put in its appearance, and luck burst like a star-rocket. The overnight guest became head of a corporation with a substantial advertising account, which he placed with Mr. B.'s concern, thus resolving Mr. B.'s economic worries.

Obviously, zest and generosity were at work here, inviting favorable chances into Mr. B's life. The essential point for our present purpose, however, is the way in which this pyramid of luck was built up, step by step. In its broad outline, this is far from being a unique experience. It is an unmistakable fact of many, and perhaps most, lives that the large fulfillments come not at a steady pace but by sudden leaps. Life's satisfactions will go along on one level for a long while, and then without warning jump upward or slip downward to another level. The greater of the upward leaps usually occur at the points of life where two or three lucky chances connect with each other.

To expect an interlocking chance at any given time, or to take reckless risks in the hope of pyramiding one's luck, would of course be folly. But after a single lucky chance, we are wise to keep all of our senses alert for other chances that may interlock with it, and so provide a major turning point of life.

This conscious effort to be alert to chance seems to be especially productive of turning points in periods of pronounced social change, such as wars. People are then shuffled around like cards in a deck, and more elements of chance are introduced into the lives of millions. While a major war is obviously a brutal tragedy whose consequences none can wholly escape, at the same time the speeding up of the play of chance produces extraordinary strokes of good, as well as bad, luck. Thus, we have a former WAC private stating that war had brought her everything she dreamed of—adventure, travel, a career, love. At another level, there are the cases of Generals Ulysses S. Grant and William T. Sherman—both failures before the Civil War, famous thereafter. Without the chances presented by World War II, it is highly doubtful that Dwight D. Eisenhower, for all his abilities, could have risen in a few years from lieutenant colonel to five-star general. Whenever chance is speeded up by exceptional social conditions, there is every reason to maintain a high degree of alertness for the luck-pyramids that can mean so much to happiness.

DON'T DESPISE SMALL CHANCES

Even in wartime, however, it would obviously be absurd to count heavily on interconnected chances to make us lucky. Only a few people, after all, have such spectacular opportunities as mark the career of an Eisenhower. War or no war, most of us go for years at a time without any but ordinary chances. It is vitally important to realize that minor isolated chances can also be productive of significant luck. To ignore such chances in the hope of something more sensational is unwise. Even though interlocking chances and important strokes of luck may never present themselves, we can often go far to make ourselves lucky by alertness to the stream of life as a whole. Respect for small, separate chances has aided some people, who lacked exceptional gifts, nevertheless to win a cumulative reputation for dependability, and to wind up as greater favorites of fortune than men of brilliant talents but erratic behavior.

We see this point illustrated in the experience of two young men, who both went to work as reporters for a Chicago newspaper at about the same time, and who had a strong sense of personal rivalry. One of these men, much the better writer of the two, began his career with a success. Assigned to cover the story of a lost child, he turned in an exceptional human interest report which brought him approval and encouragement from his city editor. Now he began to look for opportunities to distinguish himself further. When he had an assignment that seemed to give him scope for his talents, he worked hard at it; but when it seemed to him to be routine, he made little effort beyond getting the superficial facts on paper.

Here he failed to allow for the fact that in journalism many apparently routine assignments have hidden possibilities. It was when the reporter failed to be alert to a minor chance that misfortune broke around him. A gambler was arrested by a detective for operating a floating crap game. The reporter brushed the story aside as a petty police-court case and failed to question either detective or criminal. But a rival newspaper interviewed both and developed a major scoop, exposing sharp animosity between two police factions, one of which was giving protection to widespread illegal gambling in the city. The ambitious young reporter was promptly called on the carpet by his editor. This one failure offset his earlier successes in the eyes of his superiors, and dashed his hopes of early promotion.

Meanwhile, the other reporter had from the beginning been turning in fairly good stories—lacking in brilliance, not outstanding, but consistently competent. His assignments were, if anything, less stimulating than his more talented rival's. Because he took all of them seriously and because his work was not subject to wide swings in quality, he developed a reputation for sound performance; and when later an opening came for an assistant city editor, he was selected for the job.

Enthusiasm for the spectacular and impatience with the commonplace chances of life are likely to result in peaks of good luck alternating with deep valleys of misfortune. Those subject to such sharp and demoralizing swings seldom have opportunity to build on their previous good luck. It is among them that one finds men who are frequently obliged to start over in life, or who dwell sadly on past glories. A special talent or a brilliant mind can help to produce high satisfactions, but it cannot substitute for alertness to the chances that life brings us, as they come. The reservoir of luck in each of us is far more often tapped by chance in frequent little jets than in big bursts.

KEEPING ALERT FOR CRUCIAL CHANCES

Whatever the shape of the favoring chances which come our way—whether a turning point after a run of bad luck or a sudden burst of fortune or a slow accretion of lucky benefits—we cannot afford to slump into an inferior pattern of behavior after being visited by good luck. Or bad luck. To "give way to great rejoicing or great lamentation," to dwell on our hopes or fears at the expense of the external situation, would be to weaken the alertness on which our happiness may depend. Fortunately, there are specific means by which we can go far to keep ourselves alert at the times when events crowd in on us. A vivid illustration of these means is to be seen in an episode from the life of Napoleon Bonaparte, a man whose good luck for a time was almost beyond belief.

In the year 1799, while his career was still in the ascendant, Napoleon, then in Egypt, found himself in a perilous position. A British fleet under Admiral Nelson had cut him off from all communication with France; while his military position deteriorated, he was forced to operate for almost a year without any contact with the French government. Then occurred one of those apparently minor incidents on which the great dramas of history so often seem to hinge.

An exchange of prisoners took place between the British and the French, and during negotiations, as an act of courtesy, the British commander in Palestine, Sir Sidney Smith, sent Napoleon a file of English newspapers. There he read startling news: the Directory then governing France was about to fall. Eager to drop the Egyptian adventure before it ruined him, Napoleon recognized that he needed to get back to France before some new government, composed of his enemies, should take over. Only chance could help him—and it would have to be a chance that would move Admiral Nelson's fleet out of his way.

With his immense energy and bold imagination, to conceive of such a chance was to act in preparation for it. He gave secret orders: a small, fast boat was to be readied for a crossing to France; he was to be informed immediately of the slightest change in the positions of the British warships off the coast. Then he waited—but not long. A naval officer reported an unexpected shift in the pattern of Nelson's blockading fleet. Now Napoleon's alertness showed its luck-power. With nightfall he was on board his craft, setting a course that took advantage of the temporary gap in the blockade; and after a narrow escape, he arrived in France at precisely the right moment to make his successful bid for supreme power in the government.

Here was a spectacular demonstration of the truth of Shakespeare's familiar lines:

> There is a tide in the affairs of men, which
> Taken at the flood, leads on to fortune;
> Omitted; all the voyage of their life
> Is bound in shallows and in miseries.

The alertness that enabled Napoleon to take the tide at the flood was founded, as has been suggested, on three points—energy, imagination, preparation. We do not have to be Napoleons to draw the inference for our own luck-development. To keep ourselves alert in the face of crucial chances, we need, first and foremost, to maintain our *physical energy* at a high level. A sound regimen of diet, sleep, and exercise helps to assure the ability of our nerves and muscles to come quickly to the required state of tension. Beyond this, we can generate alertness through *imaginative anticipation*. While it would be obviously absurd to spend our time trying to imagine all of the eventualities of life, we can often decide in advance what we shall do if certain common chances befall us. In this way, by putting our brain on notice, we help it to recognize an emerging situation so that it swiftly sends to our nerves and muscles the impulse necessary to induce tension. Finally, when the occurrence of a chance seems fairly probable, a single *preparatory action* can go far to maintain the essential tension and keep us alert until the event takes place.

2

OUR DESIRES AND OUR LUCK

"Hope deferred maketh the heart sick;
but desire fulfilled is a tree of life."

PROVERBS

Like an invisible television antenna, the quality of alertness reaches up for the wave of chance and catches it as it passes. Before the clear image can show on the screen of our fortunes, however, many another part in the set must come into play. Essential among them is the factor of self-knowledge, with a twofold role in luck-reception. In order to be sure that any chance is favorable for us, we need to know, first, that it offers us something we really want and, second, that we have "what it takes" to respond successfully. How to develop knowledge of our real desires and knowledge of our true abilities is a question that cuts deep into the subject of luck-development.

Out of hundreds of stories of good and bad luck told by

veracious men and women emerges this unmistakable inference: The man who clearly knows what he wants out of life and what he is willing to risk for it has a far better chance of being lucky than those who are confused about their desires and ambitions. We see this principle illustrated in a boyhood incident once described by Thomas Alva Edison. At the age of fourteen, Edison earned a few dollars a week for his impoverished family by selling newspapers and other reading material on the railroad between Saginaw, Michigan, and Detroit. Passing through the train one afternoon, and calling his wares, he saw a well-dressed gentleman accompanied by a colored servant, who was carefully guarding a half-empty bottle of whisky.

"Paper, sir?" said Edison.

The traveler examined Edison from head to toe and said with a Southern drawl, "Tell me, boy, how many papers you got there?"

Edison, a little bewildered, counted his newspapers and said, "Forty."

"All right," said the Southerner. "Throw them out of the window, and then maybe we'll have some quiet around here."

Startled as he was, Tom's young mind instantly began to assess the strange chance that had befallen him. He was an ambitious boy, and more than anything else he craved education, particularly in science, which already dominated his interests. But education meant books, and he could not buy the books he wanted without a lump sum which he had never been able to save from his scanty earnings.

He did not think of all this at the time, of course, but he knew what he wanted. It flashed through his mind that here was a chance to get it. While he could not be sure of the man's intentions, he hesitated only a moment before flinging his papers, with a flourish, out of the moving train.

The Southerner nodded approvingly and said to his servant, "Pay the boy for his papers."

Pocketing a dollar, Edison went back to the car where his stock was stored. It was evident to him that the prodigal Southerner wanted no hawking of merchandise around him, and was in a mood to pay for his whim. Soon Tom was going through the train again, this time selling magazines. As he approached the Southerner's seat, he raised his voice:

"Magazines! All the latest magazines."

The man, a little drunker by now, looked at him and said, "Boy, how much are those magazines worth?"

"Six dollars," said Edison promptly.

"All right. Throw them out of the window!" He watched Edison obey, and told the servant to pay him.

The third time Edison came through the car he carried

the most expensive part of his stock, adventure stories and novels. Again the Southerner stopped him, ordered him to throw them out, and saw that he was paid.

"Let's see," the open-handed gentleman said then. "You got any more stuff out there?"

Tom confessed that his stock was gone. "All I've got left is an empty suitcase."

"Well," commanded the Southerner, "bring that and throw it out of the window."

According to Edison's own account, the money he made through that stroke of luck enabled him to buy the books which launched him into serious study of electrical science. The point of interest to us here is of another kind. It is this: Edison's mind was ready to recognize and deal with the chance because, even though very young, *he understood his own psychological requirements*. Consequently, when chance offered him an opportunity to fulfill the most urgent of those requirements, he seized it quickly.

HOW THE READY MIND
SELECTS THE RIGHT CHANCE

There is no reason to believe that opportunity knocks only once, but whether it knocks once, twice, or ten times, only the self-knowing mind, the mind that knows what it wants and what it will risk, is likely to recognize the real nature of the chance and act accordingly. Often the claims of competing desires are so strong as to make decision much more difficult than in the case of Edison. No matter how complex the problem presented by chance, a firm set of values for our various desires helps us to find the lucky answer.

By testing chances against our personal set of values we sometimes perceive luck where others are sure there is none. A case in point is that of a New York career woman whose talent and good looks had enabled her to rise in a few years to an executive position in a leading department store. Enjoying her work and prestige, she regarded romantic attachments realistically, and showed little interest in marriage. One morning this young woman stumbled as she stepped out of a taxicab and was saved from a fall by a man who chanced to be passing. Later, they saw each other in a restaurant, he spoke, she found him attractive, and they talked. She learned that he was a lawyer in a small Connecticut town, visiting New York on business.

It came as a shock to her friends when, a month later, she gave up her highly paid job, her sophisticated environment, and her active social life in order to marry this man who had spent most of his life living quietly in a setting utterly different from any she had known. Manhattan's gossips pityingly prophesied that the marriage could not last. Her reply was that she wanted a deeper fulfillment from life than her career, her romances, and her social activities had afforded, agreeable though they were. Her self-analysis was right; in the course of years the marriage proved an outstanding success, and as wife and mother she gained a deep-rooted serenity she had never known. Her luck was due not only to the chance of meeting her husband but in equal measure to the fact that she knew what she wanted and how much she was willing to give up in order to get it.

THE TEN BASIC DESIRES

In every aspect of living, the same principle holds good: *The person who knows the relative importance, for himself, of his conflicting desires is best prepared to recognize the favorable chance as it passes and to transform it into luck.* To establish priorities for one's desires is not always easy, but no one who wants to bring more luck into his life can afford to shirk this task of self-exploration. Fortunately, modern psychology has greatly clarified the problem. It tells us that the desires of man are not fixed and rigid; that, on the contrary, they are malleable, ever-changing, evolving in us from the cradle to the death-bed; and that all of them are rooted in the primal urge to live. In the infant the simple instinctive desire to remain alive expresses itself in the way he seeks the mother's breast, cries for the attention of his parents, and is frightened by the new and unfamiliar. The years of childhood bring an elaboration of infantile desire, with vague promptings toward sexual fulfillment and assertions of power. In adolescence, certainly by its end, the individual normally arrives at a developed set of adult desires, which at bottom represent the same inescapable need to feel secure in life that prompts the behavior of the newly born infant.

Of these adult desires, ten seem universal enough to justify the term "basic":

Desires which affect our sense of security largely through our relations with other people:

1. Love, particularly from those for whom we feel love, and including the affections of friendship and family life
2. Procreation, with the urge to sexual intercourse, marriage, and children as its direct expressions
3. Group status, or a firm place in a community or group, which is normally essential to the feeling of security
4. Prestige, or recognition by others of our importance and success

Desires which affect our sense of security largely through our inner life:

5. Economic security, in the sense of freedom from money worries, and a satisfying standard of living
6. Self-respect, or a sense of living up to meritorious standards of behavior
7. Self-expression, or use of one's abilities and talents, expressed in achievement or in power over others
8. Faith, or belief in a universal purpose or goal outside ourselves, from which we draw a feeling of hope and security

Desires which affect our sense of security largely through chances of heredity and physical environment:

9. Long life, or more specifically, the prospect of a long period of mental and physical vigor
10. Good health, in the sense of freedom from illness.

These are the parent desires of all our wants, ambitions, hopes, dreams, and lusts. Whenever we feel that we have been lucky, it is because chance—whether operating through others, within ourselves, or in our environment—has brought us closer to fulfillment of one or more of the ten basic desires. Merely by identifying these desires within ourselves, and understanding their common origin in the instinctive urge to live, we take a step in luck-development. It is, however, only a preliminary step. Our need now is to determine which of these ten desires deserves the higher priorities in our responses to chance—which are the more important to our happiness, which the least. Only this knowledge can qualify us to tell a potentially lucky chance from an unlucky one.

THE PERSONAL BLEND OF DESIRE

Since one man may want what another scorns, the evaluation of our desires is necessarily a highly personal matter. Everyone has, in effect, a private blend of desire. Some want more love than others, some more prestige, some more economic security, and so on. This difference profoundly affects our ideas of what is lucky. Most of us, to take the most obvious example, would consider it lucky to find a thousand dollars. But not so a certain millionaire who suffers from an obscure skin disease. To him, another thousand dollars means nothing, but he would be made intensely happy if he were to read in his morning paper that some doctor had discovered a cure for his ailment. That would be real luck for him, while, to the rest of us, such a discovery would be no more than a remote, impersonal chance.

Although variations in the personal blend of desire are

infinite in number, there are certain general characteristics which we can take into account, such as the difference in the wants between men and women, and in different age groups. The young girl is strongly affected by the desires for love, group status, and self-expression, whereas, as Dr. Kinsey's famous study shows, it is in the middle or late thirties that the typical woman's sexual urge is at its peak. In the young male, however, the dominant desire is normally sexual, thereafter yielding place gradually to the desires for economic security, power, and prestige. With maturity, the desires for self-respect and faith operate ever more strongly in both sexes.

As each individual strives to determine just what luck means to him, he needs to recognize that his set of values cannot be borrowed wholesale from a parent or from any other person, but must be worked out in terms of his own age, sex, and individuality. He must, furthermore, consider that the personal blend of desire is not a static thing, but rather is in a state of constant flux. The question that confronts everyone may be stated about as follows: "Among the various desires that I feel strongly in myself at this period of my life—and making allowance for the fact that these desires are bound to change—which of them am I willing to subordinate in order to gratify others?"

Are we, for example, willing to accept a chance which might help us to increase our power over others if by so doing we run the danger of losing affection? Shall we pass up opportunities to make money if they demand that we sacrifice health? Such difficult questions, of utmost importance in the recognition of favorable chances, can be answered luckily only if we know a good deal about our personal blend of desire.

More than superficial judgments are needed here. We need to be able to distinguish honestly between basic desires and those neurotic distortions of desire which often masquerade as genuine wants. The personal blend of desire is a delicate and sensitive balance, easily thrown out of kilter. The moment we allow false weights to tip our scale of values, we diminish our ability to appraise lucky chances accurately when they come our way. Notably, we need to be on our guard against two luck-killers—*obsession* and *frustration*—twin forces of psychic evil which are ready always to perform incalculable destruction in our lives the moment we relax our vigilance. To keep them under firm control is, as we shall see, an essential precaution in luck-development.

THE UNLUCKINESS OF OBSESSION

Ralph Waldo Emerson once wrote that we make ourselves rich by reducing our wants; and the counsel goes to the very heart of the problem of deciding what is lucky for us.

For if we do not master our wants, they are likely to end by mastering us. Like a child, every desire needs a certain amount of discipline based on understanding. To overindulge a desire is as dangerous as to repress it entirely. The saying "You can't get too much of a good thing" is a trap for the weak and foolish. Given its way, unchecked, any desire tends to swell into obsession and to destroy our luck.

We have all seen men who became alcoholics by imperceptible degrees, beginning with a drink now and then, moving on to a drink or two every evening, coming to want several drinks in the afternoon, until they were mastered by the habit. Another familiar example is the woman who begins married life with a modest wardrobe and a desire to make a good appearance, and who ends by becoming a clothes-hog and wrecking her husband's finances and her own peace of mind. Wherever we find a person driven by what Shakespeare called "that satiate yet unsatisfied desire, that tub both filled and running," we have reason to predict bad luck unless he can conquer his obsession. Like a flawed window-pane, obsession gives lunatic lines to all of life, and prevents us from recognizing luck as it passes outside our door. A motion picture director has told that when he first went to Hollywood he was thrilled by the chance to be an anonymous assistant to a famous producer, but three years later, as a full-fledged director, he ate his heart out because he thought he was being given inferior stories and inferior actors to work with. "It got so," he later confessed, "that I would not look at a story that wasn't by a name, or an actor who wasn't box-office. One day a script came down by a fellow I had never heard of. I tossed it into my outgoing basket. It went out, all right, and wound up on another director's desk. Turned out to be one of those things—a natural. He made it for peanuts with a lot of unknown kids in the cast, and he got an Oscar for it. I could have killed myself." Obsessed with a need for recognition, he was blind to the very chance that might have enabled him to realize his ambition.

While it is unquestionably true that it is the people with ambition who get things done, there is a world of difference between the normal ambition, aimed at the fulfillment of a basic desire, and the obsessing ambition, which is unfulfillable and fundamentally unlucky. The notion that people have to be consumed with ambition in order to turn out good work has no grounding in fact. There is such a thing, of course, as creative frenzy—possession by an idea—known to most artists and serious workers in every field, but this is a matter of concentration on real achievement, not of obsession with an illusory desire. If we deceive ourselves about the gratifications that our work will bring us, we are living in cloud-cuckoo land,

and are likely to tumble painfully to earth. The man who approaches his work realistically, who likes it, considers it useful, and does not expect excessive reward from it, is likely to get more and better work done over the long run than those who have to be sustained by illusion. Only the ambition which grows out of our true needs, within the framework of a balanced blend of desire, is likely to bring enduring luck into our lives.

LUCK AND THE MONEY OBSESSION

Often the runaway ambition has no basis whatever in the actual needs of its victim, but is a disguised expression of some frustrated want of the past that has gone underground. Psychiatrists' offices are full of people who, as infants, did not feel sufficiently loved to give them a sense of security and who, as adults, are neurotically obsessed with the pursuit of some desire which they can never satisfy since it merely masks the deep, forgotten frustration of the child. Many of these unfortunates are pitilessly driven by a gross appetite for power; others suffer from the need to know more than anyone else; while perhaps the most common form of the neurotic distortion of desire is money-lust. Here the normal urge to economic security is no longer in question. Money in itself becomes the greatest of all goods, for which no sacrifice of love, friendship, reputation, or health is too great.

This type of obsession bears so heavily on the luck of many thousands of people that it is worth our while to consider it in some detail. Extreme cases of money-lust are not infrequently reported in the press, such as the death of a miser who has hidden in a garret and sacrificed every normal pleasure of existence rather than spend his dollars. In quite comfortable homes, as well, one often sees men and women who subordinate every other fulfillment in order to accumulate dollars beyond need. And a many times larger number of people with modest bank accounts and incomes make themselves miserable with envy and emulation of those who have more.

Victims of the money-obsession seldom stop to ask themselves whether they can *afford* to make a great deal of money—whether the sacrifices of living demanded by the single-minded pursuit of wealth are justified by the result. Equating happiness with money, watering the word "luck" down to the point where it has only cash values, these bedeviled persons spend half their lives daydreaming of marvelous chances of the business world, the stock market, or the horse race which, without effort on their part, will lift them out of their rut to the pinnacle of wealth. While they daydream, chances which might bring them deep fulfillments of other desires—love, friends, self-respect—pass them by unnoticed. At the same time, their distorted set of values, standing in the way of judgment, exposes them to misfortune. It is in this group that one finds the favorite prey of the confidence man, the professional speculator and crooked gambler, for the eagerness to "get rich quick" makes men soft and vulnerable when their greed is appealed to.

Often the obsessed person may realize that important aspects of his emotional life are being frustrated by his compulsive desire, but this does not mean that he masters it. Sometimes he seeks help from a psychiatrist; more often he wretchedly resigns himself to his misery or perhaps tries to shrug it away. Thus, many a rich man has reassured himself that all was well with his life since he could write out a check for six figures. "I may not be loved," he tells himself, "but I am rich. I may not be popular—but I am rich. I may not be famous—but I am rich. I may be a heel—but I am rich." Among the unlucky men of wealth who think in this way one finds a significant number of suicides, insanities, nervous breakdowns, and ulcerated stomachs.

What is worse, people who suffer from the money-obsession all too often transmit it to their children, like a hereditary disease. Many a parent who believed that he was devoted heart and soul to the security of his child has known no better than to give a purely economic meaning to the word. Money, to be sure, is a useful asset in helping to make children feel secure. Although wealth does not mean happiness, acute poverty can give rise to anxieties which lead squarely to unhappiness. The child from a comfortable home undoubtedly has a somewhat better than average chance of growing up with a cheerful, confident outlook, which contributes both to worldly success and to the enjoyment of life. Even so, however, it is apparent that money can in no way guarantee the child's luck. Many insecure youths have come out of wealthy homes. The richest of parents may invite hard luck for his children by giving them the feeling that the making of money takes precedence over important psychological values. He could hardly do worse if he purposely worked to produce misfortune, for he has laid the groundwork for obsession.

PROTECTING LUCK AGAINST FRUSTRATION

All experience tells us that *it is profoundly unlucky to risk frustration of any basic desire merely to pamper another which is already adequately fulfilled,* that over the long run our happiness depends, not on the fulfillment of any one desire, but on a successful balance among all of them. Even if nine of the ten basic desires are well satisfied, the frustrated tenth can lead to bad luck. An illuminating case is that of a man living in a small rural community, with every advantage of life except one—sexual gratification, for his wife, whom he loved, was paralyzed. Frustration drove him to the city, where he struck up an acquaintance with a strange woman in a bar. Normally he was an intelligent man, but now, in his sex-hunger, he failed to recognize the signs of the professional harpy—and he wound up by falling a victim to a vicious racket, paying blackmail to spare his wife's feelings. Here we have the characteristic pattern of the intertwining of chance with frustration to produce bad luck—because *the frustration prevented a clear-sighted appraisal of the chance.*

In order to provide a firm foundation for the lucky life, we need to try to gratify every basic desire at the minimum level necessary to prevent frustration. Let us grant at once that this is not easy to do. We live in a fast-moving society which puts heavy emphasis on the pleasures of material possession and conspicuous consumption. Today youth grows up with an ever-enlarged void of unfulfilled desire for a great many well-publicized things, from automobiles to the latest in cosmetics, from lavish homes to glamorous lovers. Under this pressure, it is easy to feel a sense of frustration of our desires for a high standard of living, economic security, and prestige. We spare ourselves much pain if we recognize the probability, and normality, of a degree of frustration in life. Our problem is to prevent inevitable frustrations from distorting our set of values and warping our personal blend of desire into an unlucky pattern.

The best protection against frustration can be summed up in the word "compensation"; and we see this saving principle at work in many a life-story. The case of a recently married young man, drafted into the Army and separated from his wife, offers a significant clue to the way in which we can compensate for frustrations beyond our control.

"It was pretty bad," he wrote, "being away from Helen for months at a time, but there was nothing I could do about it. I tried not to think about how much I missed her. To take my mind off myself I decided to do some studying, which I figured was also the best thing I could do for her sake. I enrolled in an extension course in Business Administration. That has turned out to be a break. There is another fellow in my company taking the same course, and we got to know each other pretty well. His father owns a big chicken farm near Philadelphia, and they have money. I met his father when he came down to the camp. They have worked out a scheme for a big retail business in the city, direct from the farm to the consumer. They will need somebody to help run the city end, and they both say that when this is over, they will give me a crack at the job, with the promise of a piece of the business if I make good. As much time as we can manage, we work out the details and try to see the snags, and I write Helen about it regularly. It has made a big difference in the way she and I both feel."

The young man had a choice between yielding to his feelings of frustration, with self-pity, morbid introspection, and attempts at artificial escapes, or compensating for the frustration by seeking to satisfy another important desire. He chose the wise and lucky course, and in this way maintained a healthy balance of mind—which, in turn, was of prime importance in bringing him a favorable chance and an accession of hope.

It is lucky to know what we want. It is luckier still not to want too much. And it is luckiest of all to be able to compensate constructively for our unfulfilled desires while at the same time keeping our vision clear for the favoring chance that may put an end to the frustration.

3

OUR ABILITIES AND OUR LUCK

"Into what dangers would you lead me,
Cassius, that you would have me seek into
myself for that which is not there?"

SHAKESPEARE

To know whether a given chance offers something you really want is one thing. To know whether you are capable of responding to it successfully is another. One of the major elements in appraising the luck-content of a chance can be expressed in the question: Does it accord with my abilities? If it does, the probability of luck is greatly increased; if not, acceptance of the chance carries a dangerous potential of bad luck. Unless our estimate of our abilities is realistic, we can hardly help being tempted by chance into foolhardy and disastrous ventures.

Make the most of what you are and do not try to be more than you can be is part of the basic formula for the lucky life. The man who tries to live beyond his capacities, psychological, physical, or economic, invites misfortune. For even if he has favorable chances, even if ready-made good luck comes to him, he cannot sustain it. This is an obvious point, but a remarkably large number of otherwise intelligent people persistently overlook it. The case histories of men who have come to grief trying to be more than they could be make a thick file. They range through all walks of life, from the man who jumped at a highly paid job for which he was not qualified, was fired within two months, and forced at last to take a job inferior to his old one, to the young prizefighter who ambitiously let himself be over-matched and was beaten into a punch-drunk wreck in a single bout; from the woman who married a drunkard in the belief that she could reform him, and herself wound up in a sanitarium, to the Georgian prince who married an immensely wealthy girl, found himself in an unaccustomed world of yachts and high-powered automobiles, and was killed trying to prove his mettle by driving a racing car over a Spanish mountain range.

Perhaps the most revealing story showing the relationship of ability to luck is that of W. C. Durant, founder of the General Motors empire and one of the titans of American business half a century ago. His extraordinary career rests on two turning points, in both of which luck played a large part. The first came before the day of the automobile, when he was a young man with no money and no job, but with the conviction that he was a born salesman. He wanted a job selling a good product—it did not much matter what so long as it was one that people would buy. One day he went out to a small Michigan town to talk to the manager of a nearby plant, only to find when he got there that the opening had been filled. As he was dejectedly trudging back to the railroad station, a two-wheeled cart came along, and the driver offered him a lift. Durant commented on the cart, of a make that he had never seen before: it was light, strong, easy-riding, well-designed, with sleek, fashionable lines. The driver told him it was manufactured locally, and at once it occurred to Durant that *there* was a product he could sell. Instead of going back to the railroad station, he headed for the cart factory.

It turned out to be a ramshackle building with a sign outside: *For Sale.* Durant found the owner, who received him indifferently. No, he didn't want a salesman. He was selling out. Business was terrible. Yes, he had advertised the carts, but it hadn't done any good. Durant looked at the ads, and saw that they lacked imaginative appeal. His feeling grew that with intelligent promotion the cart could be sold in large quantities. Although he lacked capital, he had an even more important asset—a persuasive tongue. In an hour he had talked the owner into giving him an option on the factory and the manufacturing rights for the cart. He had recognized a chance that accorded with his basic desires and his appraisal of his abilities, and he was determined to pursue it.

A wealthy man named Dort agreed to go into partnership with Durant. Between them they took over the factory and quickly built up a highly profitable business, with Durant as chief salesman. Later, with the development of the automobile, Durant moved naturally into the new field, which he sensed would pay large rewards for selling ability. Soon he was a leading figure of the young automobile industry, and a man of great wealth. When the General Motors combine was formed, he took a leading part in promoting it, and became its first president.

So far, in all of his enterprises he had concentrated largely on promotion, salesmanship, and sales management. Now, in his new role, he found himself in a dizzy and exciting world of high finance, with enormous bond and stock deals to be undertaken, and with unprecedented chances to make—and lose—millions in stock-market speculation. At this stage the curve of his career suddenly dips downward. According to men intimately associated with him, Durant was not temperamentally qualified to dig into the intricacies of a balance sheet or a stock syndicate agreement, nor had he grasped the subtleties of stock price manipulation, as practiced in Wall Street. He began to take chances which demanded abilities that he lacked, and soon, without his quite knowing how it happened, he found himself compelled to sell a large part of his holdings in a falling market, and was forced out of the presidency of General Motors.

Subsequently, a Wall Street acquaintance came to him with a scheme for regaining control of the company. To Durant, the chance appeared favorable, but he had again misjudged his abilities. The attempt cost him the remnants of his fortune; and the tragic knowledge of failure haunted him until his death.

REQUIREMENTS VERSUS ABILITIES: A MAJOR PROBLEM OF LUCK

Durant was an able man, and he failed; but we have all seen men far less intelligent and talented who have succeeded spectacularly. What makes them lucky, while the Durants of the world are broken by fortune? In some cases, the reason for the good luck of blunderheads may lie in the very limitation of their intelligence or experience. Mark Twain once said that the formula for success was ignorance plus confidence, and there is a certain amount of truth in this satirical comment. Many men have undoubtedly taken long chances and scored successes because they did not have enough knowledge or imagination to anticipate the dangers of their enterprises. But one thing they had to have in order to succeed—ability.

The way in which a latent ability can rescue a person from the consequences of recklessness is suggested by the experience of a woman airplane pilot. She relates how, after her first flying lesson, when she hardly knew the names of the controls, her instructor was called away, leaving her alone in the grounded plane with the motor idling. On impulse, to show off, she decided to take the plane up alone. She did, and brought it down again safely, if haphazardly. Now, with many hours of solo flying time to her credit, she says feelingly, "When I think of the chance I took then, I shudder."

It should be noted, however, that whereas this woman had not understood the requirements of the chance at the start, *she had to show the necessary abilities before she was back on the ground*. Mark Twain himself gave proof that when the requisite abilities are lacking, a confident man who misjudges the requirements of a chance is begging for trouble. When chance brought to his attention the plans for a new automatic type-setting machine, his enthusiasm ran away with him, and he agreed to back its manufacture.

The result was that which often overtakes the artist who fancies himself a man of business and who seizes chances requiring abilities he has never possessed: bad luck and financial disaster.

The more a man knows about the requirements and hazards of a given chance, the more likely he is to find good luck in it, and avoid bad luck—*if he has a realistic understanding of his own abilities and limitations.* Nothing is more fruitful of good luck than the chance which accords with desire and ability; nothing more dangerous than the chance which appeals to desire not backed up by the requisite ability. To be sure, one way to get a realistic perception of one's abilities and limitations is through trial and error. But it is easy to be misled by the old saw, "You can't tell what you can do until you try." The point of diminishing returns in buying self-knowledge through failure sets in early. Many people, moreover, refuse to learn even from sad experience. Everyone has seen unfortunates who blindly continue to butt their heads against stone walls when they lack the ability to jump over—who seem to feel that if they only keep trying, they will miraculously bring forth gifts and talents they never had.

On the other hand, some people have undoubtedly missed good luck because they *under*estimated their abilities, relative to the requirements of a chance. Intensive study of a subject can sometimes cause us to see its difficulties out of proportion, and so lose confidence in our ability to cope with them.

So easy a task as boiling an egg can be made to sound formidable if we think about it in too much detail. A chef once remarked, quite seriously, "People say that anyone can boil an egg. That is true, only in the sense that anyone can put an egg into hot water and take it out again. It is false if the egg is to be eaten with enjoyment. Most customers like their eggs medium-boiled, with the yolks soft and whites firm. To achieve this result consistently is no easy matter. You must put enough water in the pan to cover the egg. You must put in the egg only after the water is boiling. Before immersing the egg, you must hold it under hot water, so that it will not crack when put into the boiling water. You must estimate the size and temperature of the egg before immersion, and regulate the time of immersion accordingly—between 3½ and 4½ minutes. After removal from the pan, to prevent further cooking in the shell, you should hold the egg briefly under cold water. Then you must serve at once. It takes a good man to boil an egg." All this may be so, and yet a man who allowed himself to be deterred from boiling an egg because of this imposing list of requirements would obviously be cheating himself out of his breakfast.

DANGER OF THE IMAGINED CAPACITY

Apparently formidable tasks often become relatively easy in the doing—*provided the essential ability is in the doer.* And abilities can be developed, if they are latent in the man. Many a person has a general capacity for a certain type of work, without ever having developed the specific abilities required. A plumber, for example, without experience in masonry, responded to an emergency request that he repair the foundation of a sagging house. After a fumbling start, he swiftly got "the hang of it" and carried the job through with the skill of a professional mason. Having the capacity for manual construction, he was quickly able to develop a new craft when chance exposed him to the problem.

It is because abilities often continue to develop within men until quite late in life that it is never quite fair to keep a fixed opinion of any man's potential of accomplishment without making allowance for changes in him. A character in one of George Bernard Shaw's plays makes the significant remark that the only man who understands him is his tailor, who takes his measure anew each time they meet. Too often we tend to use last year's measure to judge this year's man.

But making every allowance for our potentialities, it is dangerous to count on the undeveloped ability to see us through difficult situations. When a given chance comes our way, we can seldom stop to develop the requisite abilities; we either have them or we have not, and if we have not, and the chance involves serious risk, it is generally wise to leave it alone. The experiences of people who have accepted difficult chances when they had no more in them than an unmastered desire and a vague familiarity with some aspect of the problem generally have unlucky endings.

Characteristic is the case of a small-town minister who found himself, in his late forties, with a feeling of frustration over his failure to realize a boyhood dream of literary fame. He enjoyed books and plays, and had a wide cultural range; he handled words skillfully in writing his sermons; and it seemed to him that he ought to have been, and still could be, a successful author. True, he had never published anything, and for that matter had never written anything of importance aside from sermons, but he had made one or two tentative beginnings of stories and had roughed out the first scene of a play.

Then chance presented him with an extraordinary dramatic plot—or so he regarded it. The story hinged on the tragedy of a young woman in his congregation whose unhappy love life led her to attempted murder and to suicide. As an eyewitness to her death, he had been powerfully affected, and he saw it as the climax of an exciting three-act play, which, he told himself, would be an inevitable hit on Broadway.

At this point, chance had touched a basic and unsatisfied desire for recognition; he had next to consider whether he was qualified to write the play, or whether he would do better consciously to forego the chance and seek compensation for his frustration in other directions. Unfortunately, his self-appraisal was unrealistic. It led him to take a six months' leave of absence from his church and devote himself to the play. He found it infinitely harder to write than he had expected, and long before he finished, he had come to hate it. Only pride made him drive it through to the conclusion, and then he found that no reputable agent or producer would consider the play.

The revelation came to him that he had written a play so bad as to make it unmistakable that he was not, and never could be, a playwright. He understood too late the enormous difference between expository writing and creative art. And more than pride was hurt by his rash acceptance of a chance for which he lacked the needed abilities. When he returned to his congregation, he found that they preferred the new minister who had taken his place, and he was forced to accept a much less agreeable assignment.

TESTING FOR UNCERTAIN ABILITIES

To decide without an extensive trial whether one has a given ability, or enough of it to matter, is not always easy. Standards differ; the level of engineering ability required to repair an automobile engine is not enough to build one. Evidence which one man considers proof of ability is scorned by another. Nevertheless, there are certain rough tests for latent ability which we can rely on, and which serve a valuable purpose in helping us to evaluate the chances of life.

One of these is the test of *comparison*, and we see its application in a story from the life of Governor Alfred E. Smith of New York. When he was a young man, just beginning his political career, he was asked to speak at his first big political rally. His heart sank at the prospect, and he was tempted to find an excuse, for he did not consider himself a good speaker. Then chance brought him to a street corner where a Democratic friend of his was speaking. He knew that this friend was also to speak at the rally, and he stopped to listen. "He was so terrible," Al Smith reminisced, "that I figured if he could be a speaker, so could I." Both in providing encouragement and in chastening unwarranted pride, the honest comparison of one's own work with that of others can often go a long way toward making us realistic in our appraisal of a chance.

A second way of testing a hoped-for ability is through indirect evidence of one's effectiveness in a given field. Another noted political figure provides an illustration of this point. The late Senator James Hamilton Lewis of Illinois as a young man was offered a chance to study law, but was advised against doing so by friends and relatives. "You're smart enough," one of them told him, "but you just haven't got the presence and personality for it. You could never impress a jury." Lewis, taking stock of himself, feared that this was true. He was poor, ill-dressed, awkward and self-conscious, and his attempts to ingratiate himself with strangers were frequently rebuffed. Nevertheless, he hankered for the recognition and rewards of a successful legal and political career.

One day he was traveling on an Illinois river boat, and leaning against a low rail on deck, when it suddenly gave way and Lewis fell into the river. The boat stopped, someone threw him a rope, and he scrambled back to the deck. Now the concern of the passengers changed to laughter as they looked at the wet, bedraggled youth, and that laughter struck him to the heart. However, one of the passengers, an elderly gentleman, took pity on him, and learning that Lewis did not have a change of clothing, invited him to his stateroom. There he extracted from his suitcase some dry clothes, explaining as he did so that he had been at a wedding and had no others with him. With some dismay, Lewis found himself looking at a Prince Albert coat, striped trousers, and silk hat. The thought of the appearance he would make on deck in this regalia, and before a crowd which already regarded him as a figure of fun, was almost more than he could bear, but he saw no way out.

When he returned to the deck in his borrowed splendor, he tried to keep away from the other passengers, adopting an aloof, haughty manner. Then, as several of them passed by and looked at him without recognition, it dawned on him that they were not amused but impressed by his elegance. Before, they had seen a cheap, ready-made suit with an uncertain manner; now they saw an impressive exterior with an air of reserve; and they could not identify the man beneath. Thereafter, still maintaining his new-found dignity, he held several conversations with strangers and discovered that they seemed flattered by his affability and listened attentively to his remarks. "At that moment," said Lewis, "I realized that while clothes may not make the man, they could make the lawyer, and I resolved never to forget the lesson." His mind was made up; he studied for the bar, and from then on put all the money he could spare into his wardrobe. In his subsequent career in Chicago and Washington, he became famous for his sartorial impressiveness and for his success with juries and with voters.

WHEN TO RELY ON OTHERS' OPINIONS

The episode of the boat, casual though it was, provided Lewis with evidence of his ability to command favorable attention—enough to justify his acceptance of the chance at a legal career. Even indirect evidence of our abilities, however, is not always available to us. At such times, the opinions of others can sometimes provide a useful substitute.

Naturally, there are pitfalls to be avoided in basing one's selection of chances on outside judgment, which may be, and often is, biased. We see this danger exemplified in the case of a conscientious young woman pianist who was persuaded by a wishful family that she was a genius. Her father, a real-estate broker, was involved in the sale of a house for the manager of a leading concert hall, and in lieu of a fee he stipulated that his daughter be invited to give a recital. The manager consented to hear her play but told her frankly that he did not think she was ready for so severe a test. Her family's eagerness and her own dreams, however, carried greater weight with her; and the manager, anxious to save his brokerage fee, finally shrugged and consented to arrange the recital.

Here was bad luck in the making—the chance of the brokerage deal, impinging on the family's distorted estimate of the girl's ability. No one else was surprised when the concert was poorly attended, and the reviews savagely critical. The result was a nervous crisis for the unfortunate girl and the destruction of much of her pleasure in music.

In soliciting outside judgment of our abilities, we need to allow for the possibility that it may be warped. Nevertheless, the willingness to listen to and be guided by others' opinions about our abilities can bring great good luck—*provided that the opinions are objective*, and grow out of an understanding of the requirements of the chance. Thus, we have the case of an exuberant young man who gave up a lucrative job in New York in order to buy a Connecticut farm, which he thought would bring him independence and happiness, and into which he sank all his capital.

Some months later he and his wife discovered that it would take much better and more Spartan farmers than they to extract a living from that stony hillside. In spite of their worry, they managed to see humor in their precarious situation, and it did not prevent them from successfully entertaining the numerous friends who visited them. One of these, a businessman of much experience, said to him, "There's no place I like to visit more than yours. With your disposition and temperament you could keep hostel." Others who were present agreed. Up to that moment the young man had not considered converting his farm into an inn; now it occurred to him that if these people, whose judgment he respected, saw in him the ability to be a public host, they might be right: the same kind of reception and entertainment that had appealed to his friends might attract paying guests.

Here a lucky outcome depended on an ability highly estimated by others, even though it had never been specifically tested. In the upshot, the young farmer advertised for guests; a few came, liked the expansive atmosphere he created, and told others. Little by little the reputation of his farm as a week-end resort grew, together with his facilities, until he found that instead of being a bankrupt farmer he was a successful innkeeper, with a prosperous enterprise.

INNER CONVICTION AS A TEST OF ABILITY

Comparison—indirect evidence—the opinions of others—these three tests can help us to appraise the chances of life which call for as yet unproved abilities. There is still another test—that of *inner conviction*. Since we can easily mistake the wish for the conviction, this test obviously needs to be applied with great caution. One otherwise intelligent man spent twenty years in a state of ever-increasing depression because he had convinced himself as a youth that he was potentially a great actor, and would not heed the mounting evidence to the contrary. On the other hand, one has such cases of the value of internal conviction as that of Katharine Cornell, who as a young girl was told by an angry play director that she would "never be an actress." So strong was her certainty that her future lay on the stage that she refused to be dismayed, and a few years later the world was applauding her remarkable talents.

Where internal conviction asserts itself with sufficient power, it can often bring luck in spite of the most adverse outside judgments. The successful public relations specialist, Ivy Lee, used to laugh at himself for the advice he gave to two confident, young would-be publishers who approached him in the 1920s with a plan for a new type of news-magazine, which would put heavy stress on photographs, personalities, and a brisk, nervous, attention-demanding style. "I told them I did not think it would go," said Lee, "and I had grave doubts about their being qualified to publish a magazine. But they were completely sure of themselves—paid no attention to me—and just as well." The two young men were Henry Luce and the late Briton Haddon, and the magazine was *Time*.

On the whole, inner conviction of an ability is a reliable index to luck only when it is accompanied by deep instinctive understanding, such as one associates with great talent or genius. Too many people try to convince themselves of as yet undisclosed abilities, and take disastrous chances without any real grasp of the requirements—like the young musician who once said to Mozart, "Herr Mozart, it has been suggested to me that I write a symphony. Would you be good enough to tell me how to go about it?"

"You are young to write symphonies," said Mozart gently. "Why not try ballads first?"

Indignantly the young man replied, "You wrote symphonies when you were ten years old."

"Ah, yes," said Mozart. "But I didn't ask how."

Many a man has told himself that by "finding out how" he could accomplish wonders, and has taken chances accordingly, only to find that he did not after all have the ability to make use of the technique—that his conviction of talent was no more than the dream-product of disguised desire. *Only when a given chance conforms both to basic desire and to demonstrated or indicated ability does it give genuine promise of good luck.*

4

JUDGMENT AS AN ELEMENT IN LUCK

"I see men's judgments are a parcel of their fortunes."

SHAKESPEARE

While in estimating some chances we need only know what we want and what we can do in order to make a lucky decision, others carry an inherent element of risk, a fixed hazard that has nothing to do with us. A simple example is a poker hand, say, a four-flush. As the five cards are dealt to us, they represent a chance to be appraised. We need hardly appraise them in terms of desire, for we want to win; as for ability—we are, let us say, good players. But that does not assure us of luck. Whatever we may do, when we discard the useless fifth card and draw a substitute in the hope of completing the flush the odds are still three to one against us. *This is the inherent risk of the chance*, which we need to consider before we accept it.

To make accurate estimates of inherent risk in games of chance, such as poker, roulette, and dice, is relatively easy. The inherent risks of life as a whole are far more complex. We cannot compute risk in precise mathematical terms when we select a career, marry, or even invest our money. To increase the probability of a lucky outcome in any such chance, we need to calculate its risk before we accept it—not afterward.

When men who have scored outstanding triumphs in life speak of their luck, they tacitly convey that in taking chances, their judgment of inherent risk has proved right. Blessed with good judgment, a man dives into the uncertain wave of chance and comes up, as an Arabian proverb says, "with a fish in his mouth"; lacking judgment, he finds himself dashed on the rocks of misfortune. It is in this sense that we must regard the famous remark of the fabulously wealthy Julius Rosenwald, when he attributed his business achievements "ninety-five per cent to luck, five per cent to ability." His modesty could not conceal the fact that superlative judgment in appraising chance situations played a tremendous part in the "ninety-five per cent."

Judgment has been appropriately called the eye of the mind; while some lucky people, like Rosenwald, seem to be born with X-ray vision into life's chances, in others the mental eye is so astigmatic that it persistently leads to folly. Even people who have come to distrust their own judgment, however, can often make surprising headway in strengthening it by the application of a few simple principles. Close examination of cases of chronically bad judgment indicates that it is usually due less to defects in thinking than to emotional factors which have sneaked into the mind's outlook and given it an unlucky twist. It is against these distortions that we need to guard if we are to improve our luck. *To three unstable emotional states— boredom, anxiety, and overconfidence—many people owe an appalling amount of bad luck.* "Beware of boredom." "Allow for anxiety." "Overcome overconfidence." These rules, as we shall see, are important markers on the road to better luck.

WHY BOREDOM INVITES BAD LUCK

Boredom, it must be said at once, is not always unlucky. In fact, under the right conditions boredom figures in preparation for some of life's high satisfactions. One does monotonous finger exercises in order to learn how to play the piano; we read even the most tedious passages of the Bible, Plato, and Dante in order to receive the revelation of the whole; and husbands and wives learn to put up with a degree of boredom with each other's conversation because it is outweighed by other values of marriage. But

while boredom endured for a higher purpose can be rewarding, most boredom is not of this kind. Usually we are
bored, not so much because of our work or our environment, but because of a zestless attitude of mind. In this
condition, anything we do seems dull by comparison with
what we can imagine ourselves doing. Hungry for the
event that will lead him to a fuller life, the bored man
looks with favor on almost any chance that promises a
thrill. Thus he becomes highly vulnerable to bad luck, for
inevitably he tends to neglect the element of inherent risk
in the chances he takes.

Many people who have been pushed by boredom into
tragic misfortune are not even aware of the reason for
their trouble. A characteristic instance is that of a girl who
had left her home to run off with a married man twice her
age, and without either good looks or distinction of personality to commend him. Contrite and miserable, she
finally returned to her home and said to her shattered
parents, "I don't know why I did it. I didn't love him. I
must have been crazy." She was not crazy. She was bored.
The sad truth is that many young people drift through life
in a state of boredom so acute as to produce almost lunatic
blindness to the inherent risk of superficially exciting
chances.

Bored adults are no less prone to experience bad luck.
Many a lonely, bored man has been tempted by a new

acquaintance to disastrous risk because he was grateful to have anyone pay attention to him. In one case, reported to the New York police, a visitor to the city allowed himself to be taken in by so flagrant a confidence trick that even the unsurprisable policemen to whom he told his story shook their heads. "I knew it sounded like he was up to something," the victim admitted. "But he seemed like a pretty nice fellow, and I was so glad to have his company that I thought I would take a chance on letting him hold the money." The same psychology explains why the confidence man and gold-brick merchant flourished for so long in sparsely settled regions of the United States. Bored families were so pathetically eager to be entertained by any friendly stranger that they uncritically exposed themselves to the excitement of his fabulous promises.

Even among so-called sophisticates of our own time, the same principle holds true. A man who had lost thousands of dollars that he could not afford in a crooked gambling game gave as his reason that he was "bored with his family and friends"; recklessly eager for diversion, regardless of risk, he was an open target for bad luck. Innumerable businessmen have lost large sums of money because the monotony of their work tempted them to create excitement for themselves with injudicious speculation.

And much more than money is often lost to boredom. An Arkansas farmer hailed before a court because he had participated in a lynching told the judge that he had done it because "there wasn't anything better to do at the time." Sociologists have pointed out that the worst kinds of mob behavior, witch-burnings, pogroms, lynchings, and the like, can probably be attributed in good part to the prevailing boredom of the individuals who compose the mob. The typical member of such a mob is probably less a sadist than a bored man, who finds little entertainment in normal life. To kill without fear of reprisal and without violating the code of the community is to him a way of enlivening an otherwise humdrum existence. Even within the home the effects of boredom on human behavior are often startling in their extravagance. Men have frequently quarreled with their neighbors, beaten their wives, and taken to drink as an expression of the revolt against boredom.

We cannot safeguard our luck against boredom with entertainments or excitements. The appetite for such external escapes grows quickly jaded. Over the long run, it is only by filling our lives with interest, by the development of zest, that we protect the judgment from the pressure of boredom. There is one effective precaution, however, that even the bored man can take when he is called upon to appraise a sudden chance. That is *simply to recognize the fact that he is bored*. If he can remember to tell himself that in his bored frame of mind he cannot expect to estimate risk accurately, he may at least give himself a breathing spell, and a second look at the chance before he decides to accept it. Just as when we feel fatigued, we say to ourselves, "I am too tired to think about this now; I shall wait until my mind is refreshed," so when we feel bored, we need to admit and master our boredom before we pass judgment on chances that may vitally affect our luck.

ANXIETY AND LUCK

Similarly, in forming our judgment of chances, most of us urgently need to allow for states of anxiety. This universal by-product of a feeling of insecurity moves in devious ways to undermine our luck. We have already remarked on the power of anxiety to destroy our luck-lines and prevent us from attracting good fortune. That is only part of its menace. Anxiety actually causes us to reject favorable chances, even when they come straight at us, by making us think that we see peril and risk where there is none. "Imagining some fear," Shakespeare writes, "how easily is a bush supposed a bear." The hag-ridden imagination fills the world with nonexistent bears; the ever-anxious person, by continually exaggerating all the hazards of life, weakens judgment to the point where its light can no longer probe into the fog of uncertainty to see what really lies there. Offered promising opportunities, he hesitates, draws back, broods, worries, until the time for action is past, and the harvest he might have had is reaped by others.

In addition to repelling good luck, anxiety attracts positive misfortune by focusing our attention on imaginary risks and so distracting us from those which actually exist. To understand and guard against this unlucky treachery of the anxious mind is a matter of great moment in luck-development.

If the average housewife finds that a piece of meat recently bought has become tainted, she takes it back indignantly to the butcher, or else she throws it out, regretfully but unhesitatingly. The bad luck involved ends with the dollar or two which has been wasted. The same minor chance, however, can lead to a much more serious outcome, when judgment is distorted by anxiety. The young housewife involved in the following story was a person of considerable charm, but she was filled with neurotic anxiety. Although its origin (as was later revealed) went far back into her childhood, the trouble was intensified by the attitude of her husband, an exacting, somewhat tyrannical man. Inevitably, she went to great lengths to defend herself at all times against criticisms that she thought he might make, or had implied.

One day, upon opening her refrigerator, this young woman noticed on odd smell in the meat chest. Could it come, she wondered, from a piece of cellophane-wrapped pork, bought a few days earlier? She smelled it closely, but by now her nostrils, accustomed to the odor, could not be quite certain.

At this stage, her judgment was operating on the chance in a perfectly normal way—exploring it, estimating the risk. Immediately, however, her prevailing anxiety worked itself into her mind-process. Had she kept the meat too long? Was she guilty of inefficient household management? Would her husband criticize her? She did not, of course, formulate these questions consciously. If she had, she would have realized their folly.

So she smelled the meat again. Now she told herself that the smell was very faint—unnoticeable, really. It might have been only imagination. Certainly, the meat was not seriously spoiled. And thorough cooking would kill the germs. (Later, she said she knew that the danger of tainted meat is not always due to germs, but at the time this thought did not come to her.) Result: the pork was served at dinner that night, the entire family became seriously ill, and the woman had a severe psychological crisis. Bad luck that the pork had gone bad? No, merely an unfavorable chance. The bad luck did not result until this woman's anxiety led her to underestimate the inherent risk of a dangerous chance.

This is, of course, an extreme example; in most of us,

fortunately, anxiety is neither so continuous nor so strong. Still, few of us are free from occasional anxious states of mind. Although, in order to be lucky, we do not need to rid ourselves entirely of anxiety, *good luck does demand that in appraising the chances of life we make allowance for anxiety.* Merely by bringing the fears in our minds into the open and seeing how they are likely to affect judgment, we go some distance to offset them. Only by facing up to the fact of anxiety can we keep our mental vision clear to distinguish between lucky and unlucky chances.

PROTECTING THE SHARED LUCK OF MARRIAGE AGAINST ANXIETY

In this connection, it is important to recognize the extent to which we ourselves may be responsible for the kind of luck that befalls our marriage partner or, for that matter, anyone close to us. In the story just related we saw how a martinet-husband can fill a wife with fear—and so invite bad luck in which both share. Anxiety has an easy time driving husbands and wives, especially those who are psychologically immature, to actions damaging to the common fortunes. The wife who goes through her husband's pockets while he sleeps has figured in many a joke, but she is in fact a subject for pity; for her behavior, growing out of anxiety, carries a potential of bad luck.

It is, moreover, easy for anxiety to give rise to feelings of repressed hostility which, carrying the distortion of judgment even further, need only the slightest nudge from chance to produce misfortune for both partners. Even people who feel affection for each other, and who are fundamentally well-disposed, will frequently make those around them anxious and hostile—poisoning the common pool of luck. A typical story is told by a husband who had been married for twelve years, and whose relations with his wife up to the time of this episode were neither better nor worse than in most marriages. There came a period when pressure of business forced the husband to work late at his office on a number of evenings; but he neglected to forewarn his wife and each night she prepared a dinner which went uneaten. The feeling that he was ceasing to care for her now made her anxious; and anxiety's ugly twin, hostility, was not long in putting in an appearance.

Absorbed in his business problems, the husband brushed aside his wife's complaints. A few days later he was sarcastically told by his employer, "I understand you feel you have been working too hard."

"Not at all," said the husband. "Why do you say that?"

"That's what your wife told mine," said the employer.

That night the husband demanded of his wife, "What did you tell the boss's wife about my working too hard?"

"Why," said the wife, "we just happened to meet in a store and she asked me how you were, and I said that you were working day and night. That's all. What's wrong with that?"

The husband angrily pointed out that she had jeopardized his position with her "foolish remarks." She returned that she had merely spoken the truth. He countered by saying that he had not complained—that his hard work was only a sign that he was enthusiastic about his job. Why couldn't she have just said *that* to the boss's wife? The resulting quarrel was long and bitter, and seriously damaged their relationship.

Consciously, this woman had doubtless wanted to speak only the truth to the boss's wife, but the presence of hostility made it difficult for her to express herself without conveying more than she said. Under these circumstances, the couple were an open target for bad luck. The links in the chain are unmistakable: the husband's lack of consideration producing anxiety; anxiety giving rise to hostility; hostility warping judgment; bad judgment preventing a sound appraisal of a chance situation; and, finally, bad luck for husband and wife.

We shake our heads over the ill-fortune of a near relative or friend; yet often our own actions may have contributed to the trouble. In family life, especially, where the judgment of one person may sharply affect the luck of all, each best safeguards his own fortunes when he protects the minds of others against needless anxiety. To allow for anxiety in ourselves when we appraise life's chances is not enough; we need to watch for its signs in those close to us, and to allay it, if we can, through generous and considerate behavior.

OVERCONFIDENCE AS A LUCK-KILLER

In some ways the most important rule for protecting judgment against unstable emotions is that which we have phrased as "Overcome overconfidence." At the same time, it is a rule which many people feel does not apply to them. "Me overconfident? Certainly not! Why, if anything, my trouble is that I am not confident enough." This everyday statement represents the sincere belief of millions.

They incline to think of overconfidence in terms of the tennis champion who feels that he can take it easy against an inferior opponent, and finds himself losing. Where luck is concerned, this is the least costly form of overconfidence. Far more serious in its unlucky implications is the overconfidence which comes from three other sources: *a run of luck; misunderstanding of motive; and inexperience.* The facts show that the people who feel they lack confidence are often the very ones in whom these factors work to produce overconfident behavior, causing them to accept unlucky chances against which clear judgment would have warned them.

Nothing warps the judgment more than an unjustified sense of being lucky. When the old Romans said, "Walk warily in the sight of the smiling gods," they spoke for the ages. "This is my lucky day." "Things are breaking for me, I can't lose." Such remarks have often been the prelude to disaster for a man who has been casually favored by passing chance. A piece of luck just past usually leaves a glow of elation in our minds, like a summer rainbow—and despite myth, neither has a pot of gold at its end.

We can study in some detail the effect of the unwarranted "lucky feeling" on judgment and fortune in a dramatic example dating back to the early years of this century. It is the story of a young Englishman, John Coombe Trafford, who had a great run of luck at Monte Carlo. The facts as related by Trafford are these: When he went into the Casino, it was in his mind to risk 200 francs, then the equivalent of forty dollars. He expected to lose; all he really wanted was to be able to say that he had played the wheel in Europe's greatest gambling establishment.

As he paused at the entrance of the vast room, full of fashionably dressed people, his eye caught a glimpse of a lovely young woman, apparently alone, at one of the green roulette tables. He chose that table, and when the girl, who seemed to be French, demurely avoided his gaze, he determined to make an impression on her. It was early in the evening, and no one was playing heavily. Instead of putting down a few francs to begin, as he had intended, Trafford impulsively tossed the entire 200 francs on number 8. It was far from being a sensational bet, but it was large enough to make people look at him. As the wheel began to spin, he prepared himself for the faintly amused expression, the negligent shrug, which he felt would be appropriate when the croupier raked in the money. Those 200 francs, lost with grace, might win him a smile and open the way for conversation with his charming neighbor.

He hardly bothered to look at the wheel when he heard the ball rattle into a slot, and it was a second or two before he realized that the croupier had intoned, *"Huit, pair et noir."* An impressive stack of chips, which he realized amounted to 35 times 200, or 7,000 gold francs, was pushed toward him. He picked up a 20-franc piece and tossed it to the croupier, and as he was thanked, he looked at the girl and smiled.

She smiled in return, and a few seconds later they were talking, and Trafford was working so hard over his French that he paid no attention to the spinning wheel. A commotion at the table, a squeal from the girl, made him turn. It came to him with a shock that his original stake of 200 francs still lay on number 8, and 8 had come up again. In five minutes, in two plays, he had won 14,000 francs—$2,800.

He was a man of modest means, and a tremendous excitement shook him. The girl said, "But you must play—fortune is in your fingers." Together they stood at the table, and for four hours he was carried along on an extraordinary winning streak. Finally, with a tremendous coup, he "broke the bank"; that is to say, the wheel at that particular table was stopped for the evening, and Trafford found himself winner by 110,000 francs.

Elated, he stopped; he had no intention of risking his winnings in further play. He left the Casino, his pockets filled with money, the girl at his side, and they began to walk to his hotel, taking a short cut at her suggestion. Intent on their talk, he never saw the two men who suddenly came up behind them in a dark passage. One of them hit him over the head with a club, and when he came to, his money and the girl were both gone. For two weeks he was in the hospital with a serious concussion. There he learned from the police that the girl was a member of a gang that preyed on unsuspecting men who went to the Casino alone and chanced to win.

Had he not been made overconfident by his gambling luck, it seems reasonable to say, he would have been more cautious—perhaps banked his winnings at the Casino or hired a carriage or insisted on walking along well-lighted ways. Overconfidence, as it always does, clouded judgment. It seemed to Trafford that luck was on his side, that nothing could go wrong—and so everything went wrong, and luck was against him.

THE ELEMENT OF MOTIVE IN LUCK

On a less spectacular scale, and in many walks of life, similar experiences occur every day. So also do cases of bad luck resulting from another type of overconfidence—that which comes with the belief that we understand other peoples' motives, when we actually do not. Too many of us naïvely accept, at face value, the motives put forward by persons with whom we must deal in chance situations. An acquaintance may tell us that he offered us this or that chance because we are so clever or important or attractive or lovable. When this happens, we guard against overconfidence and protect our luck if we probe a little beneath the surface of his assurances.

Many chances, like secondhand cars, conceal unlucky risks beneath a shiny exterior. Not that we need to be cynical about the motives of other people. Cynicism is, in truth, only an inverted form of naïveté, twisting one's view of reality. Those who uniformly put the worst interpretation on other people's actions must inevitably cut themselves off from many favorable chances. At the same time, in cases where we have no reason to believe in the other person's purity of motive, we do well to pause for reflection.

A British writer tells a story which demonstrates the unlucky possibilities of failure to consider the motives of others. He was in Berlin in 1932 to gather material for articles on German politics for certain magazines to which he frequently contributed. One night while at dinner in the Adlon Hotel he was told that a reception was being given in an adjoining room and that the rising political leader, Adolf Hitler, was present. The Englishman said to his German companion, also a writer, that he was curious about Hitler, and wondered what sort of man he was. The German replied noncommittally, and excused himself. A few minutes later he came back smiling, accompanied by a Nazi officer who formally invited the Englishman to attend the reception; the Fuehrer had heard of him and had expressed a desire to meet him. Without hesitation, the Englishman accepted, feeling both grateful to his German friend and pleased that his name should be so well known in Germany.

A few minutes later he found himself shaking hands with Hitler—and then flashlights went off all around them. For the first time, he realized that photographs of this meeting, if published, would do him harm among his friends and the editors for whom he wrote. On the other hand, Hitler and the Nazis could only profit by having it appear that British liberals were seeking his friendship. The writer could do nothing to prevent it. Soon after the photographs appeared, under captions which implied that he was one of Hitler's supporters, he found that many of his former associates grew cool to him, and his reputation suffered in quarters where his professional career was involved. Speaking of the incident, he said, "What an unlucky decision that was! If only I had stopped to think why Hitler could possibly have wanted to meet me!"

GUARDING LUCK AGAINST NAÏVETÉ

The "I can't lose" feeling and the misunderstanding of motive, while seriously affecting judgment, are no more of a menace to our luck than the overconfident impulses which grow out of inexperience. Although naïveté based on lack of experience is easily forgiven in the young, it wreaks havoc in the luck of adolescents and adults alike. The inexperienced person, underestimating the requirements of success in unfamiliar aspects of life, often rushes in only to discover concealed dangers. In case after case of misfortune—the unhappy marriage, the wrecked car, the hopeless undertaking, the bankrupt business—the origin of the trouble lay in an overconfident assumption that the person concerned understood the requirements and risks of a chance, when in fact he was dangerously inexperienced.

Oddly enough, many crass examples of unlucky judgment due to inexperience come from a class popularly conceived to be hardheaded and practical—the businessman. The evidence of failures and investment losses bespeaks an appalling amount of naïveté in business circles. As for speculation, a professional and highly successful speculator in stocks has made a trenchant comment on the unlucky overconfidence of businessmen when they try to use their money to make money in stocks. He said:

"A man often thinks because he is pretty good in his own business and reads the financial news and talks with the other commuters in the train about business conditions, that qualifies him as a pretty shrewd fellow, who isn't going to get burned in the market. But he is just as vulnerable as anyone else. Unless the amateur speculator is fortunate enough to have the friendly guidance of a talented financial man, and unless he is of a temperament not to be physically ruined by tension and worry, he is looking for trouble if he tries to play the market without knowing a lot of things which most so-called investors never even know they ought to know. And you not only have to master a difficult field of knowledge. In addition, you need the qualities of character not to overextend a speculative position, to ride out a falling market if need be, and to be able to take a profit or cut a loss in time. Then you have a pretty good chance of coming out on top. Otherwise you are just a sucker."

Sometimes, as in complicated matters of investment and in business deals, it takes a long time and patient study to protect our luck against inexperience. There are, however, many chance situations in life when a telephone call or the reading of a few printed pages or a conversation with an experienced person can provide enough facts to make the difference between a lucky and an unlucky decision. Not infrequently, a wife entirely without business experience has been known to give her allegedly practical husband excellent guidance in his affairs because she asked a searching question that made him probe for more facts before saying "yes" to a proffered chance.

WHAT MAKES A LUCKY GAMBLER?

When it comes to guarding luck against inexperience and overconfidence, most of us have much to learn from the successful gambler. Contrary to a common impression, the luckiness of the professional bettor who wins consistently is usually not due either to excessive favoritism on the part of chance or to crooked "fixing." Behind the luck of the honest gambler—and many are honest—lies superior judgment of inherent risk. This quality of judgment, in turn, grows in large part out of special knowledge obtained through patient effort.

The successful gambler insures his luck. That is, he minimizes his risks by a careful study of chance situations. Generally, he feels contempt for the petty crooks of his profession who find it necessary to resort to illegal practices—loading dice, putting magnets under roulette wheels, keeping an ace up the sleeve, and bribing jockeys and ball players. His general attitude is illustrated by the testimony of the Milwaukee gambler, Sidney A. Brodson, before the Kefauver Crime Investigating Committee of the United States Senate. Brodson startled the Senators by his revelation of the businesslike methods by which he appraised the probable outcome of sporting events, as a basis for bets totaling over a million dollars a year. He had one employee whose sole job it was to read the sports pages of more than a hundred newspapers and study the form and condition of contestants. Telephone calls for information cost Brodson $15,000 annually. By knowing more than the public, he was able to perceive opportunities for bets in which the odds favored him; and he stated that he avoided events which showed signs of having been fixed, since dishonest interventions by other gamblers could ruin his calculations. It is hardly surprising that he won most of his bets.

Thomas W. Lawson, the sensational Wall Street specu-lator, once made a remark which suggests the secret of the lucky gambler. He had just emerged victorious from a titanic stock exchange battle with a powerful group of bankers, and someone asked him, "Weren't you worried?" "No," said Lawson. "They never had a chance. I was two facts ahead of them all the time." Although a successful gambler may wear a cloak of recklessness, under it he gen-erally conceals specialized knowledge which enables him to calculate inherent risk better than the next fellow.

Many people who recognize the need to guard against overconfidence in situations involving their money, and who cautiously shun bets in which the probabilities are against them, nevertheless fail to apply this principle to other hazards of life. A young man tells of a wonderful job offered to him by a comparative stranger, and for which he left other employment: how was he to know that the new company was about to go bankrupt? A businessman disgustedly relates his sad experience with a charming fellow who answered an advertisement for a job, got it, and turned out to be a thief. A young woman says, "I will never trust a man again," because one man, met under romantic circumstances, asked her to marry him, bor-rowed money from her, and then walked out of her life. In all such instances, an unfavorable chance was accepted because the person involved overconfidently took the plunge without making the slight extra effort "to find out," which might have protected judgment.

By working to overcome overconfidence, whatever its origin—by remembering to avoid crucial decisions at times of boredom and anxiety—we clear away the emotional fog that obscures our vision of life's chances.

5

SAFEGUARDING LUCK
WITH SELF-RESPECT

"Mine honour keeps the weather of my fate."

SHAKESPEARE

C hoose," life frequently says to us, "choose instantly between money and self-respect"—or it may be "between love and self-respect"—or even "between self-respect and danger." Faced with such difficult choices, only awareness of the real issues which are at stake can guide us safely to luck. And if self-respect is sacrificed—then look out! Probably no other human flaw produces so many devastating examples of bad luck as a failure in this department of the personality.

Among all the desires of men, the desire for self-respect has a unique status. All of life, every aspect of behavior, is pervaded by our need to feel that we are living up to meritorious standards of conduct. The case histories of lucky and unlucky lives uniformly point to a basic luck-principle which can be summed up in these words: *It is always unlucky to forfeit self-respect.*

The test of self-respect is especially important when chance demands an instantaneous decision and allows no time for judgment to probe or consider. While self-respect does not, of course, enter into every pressing chance, again and again it acts to give swift warning against chances which are superficially tempting but ultimately unlucky.

To tell which course of action will best maintain self-respect in a complex situation is not always easy. A woman, for example, may find herself forced to choose between living with a man she hates or leaving her home and children. Which choice will do least violence to her self-respect? No one can answer for her; the clue is to be found only in her own heart. In many another chance of life, however, the issue is clear, and we can have no doubt as to the course of action required to preserve self-respect. Our problem then is to face up to the issue squarely—to recognize that the will to maintain self-respect at all hazards is a key to the lucky life.

Everyone knows, in theory, at least, that self-respect is essential to happiness. Yet many are so insensitive to the demands of self-respect that they continually subordinate it even to the most trivial hankering, such as curiosity. How many people have surreptitiously peeped at the private papers of their friends, when they thought they would not be caught at it? For no better reason, generally, than idle curiosity to know a little more about the friend than he had told them.

Ah, you may say, but surely one does not lose much self-respect by such innocent actions. Unfortunately, the loss is greater than we generally recognize—as we see when the peeper is caught. How miserable he is then with embarrassment, how awkward it is for the friend who tries to laugh away the episode! Even when he is not detected, the man who thus tramples on self-respect pays an unlucky penalty, for fear of detection unconsciously generates insecurity feelings which sooner or later are bound to affect his behavior and injure his luck. Anyone who does not have an overruling loyalty to a noble purpose, and who allows himself to accept chances that injure self-respect, asks for eventual bad luck, in a massive dose.

DANGERS OF VIOLATING SELF-RESPECT

The example just cited is a common one; but the same principle applies in unusual and dramatic cases, where men have had to make extremely difficult choices involving self-respect. One revealing story begins with a woman's purse, left on a bench in a subway station and found by a passer-by, a reasonably intelligent, well-disposed, moderately educated and dimly religious man. These are his words:

"It wasn't stealing. Finders are keepers, after all, and I was hard up. At first the thing that bothered me was the keys and the papers. I knew she (the woman who lost the purse) would be in trouble without those. I did not see how I could send them to her without maybe making her suspicious, but at the same time I could not bring myself to throw them away. I was afraid to keep them in the apartment because I figured my wife might find them and be suspicious, and I did not want to tell her about finding the purse. I knew she would have been against my keeping the money. So I put the keys and papers in an envelope in my desk at the office. Every time I opened the drawer and saw them there it bothered me. After about two weeks, I was thinking about those keys and papers even when I was eating dinner or playing cards or trying to sleep. I told myself to forget it. It was foolish to keep thinking about it. But I couldn't seem to forget it.

"Finally I decided to mail the keys and papers back to the woman, anonymously. That worried me, too, because I figured if she went to the FBI or somebody, they might trace my fingerprints on the envelope. So I wore gloves when I put the things into the envelope and sealed it. That meant I couldn't let anybody see me do it. I stayed at the office until everybody went home, and did it, and I felt like a criminal, even though I was only trying to do the right thing. I even printed her name and address so nobody could recognize my handwriting.

"When I got home late, I caught hell from my wife and we had the worst fight we ever had. That night I hardly slept. Instead of feeling better about it I felt worse. That money worried me. I had put it into a different bank account, and I kept the bankbook at my office so my wife would not find it. I used part of it to pay some bills, and then I wondered what to tell my wife when the bills didn't come. I couldn't figure what I ought to do about reporting the money on my income tax, either. For all I know, the banks sent lists of depositors to the income tax people, and maybe they would check up on me. I was in a lousy state of mind, worried all the time. The thing was doing me harm in a lot of ways I can't describe. Little things were going wrong at the office and at home. I found myself sighing as if I had lost my best friend, and my wife said I groaned in my sleep.

"This went on for nearly a year, and I was in one hell of a shape. I kept thinking I would give back the money, what there was left. Once I went around to this woman's address to see what kind of a place she lived in, and it wasn't any better than mine. She must have had all the money she ever owned in that purse. If I could have gone to the priest and confessed and let him handle it I would have, but I hadn't been in a church for years. Finally I said to myself I would do what I knew the priest would tell me to do—give back the money I had left. It broke me up doing it, but I went to the bank and drew it all out, and I made a package out of it and sent it to her, the way I did with the keys and papers. I did not even dare to register it, and I could not be sure she ever got it, but I did make certain she was still living at that address. The whole thing was an awful experience. All I can say is that I learned a lesson, and I don't want any more lessons like that."

Possibly this man's conscience troubles had other, less visible, and deeper rooted causes, but the issue of the purse created a crisis of self-respect for him. The pattern is one which occurs again and again: first, a superficially lucky chance involving self-respect; second, failure to recognize the danger to self-respect, and acceptance of the chance; third, temporary gratification of some other desire; and fourth, sharp deterioration of the psychological state of the unlucky man. This deterioration usually shows itself in a weakening of the personality, distrust of one's judgment, and a pervasive uncertainty of action tending to damage all human relations.

Many people who experience these troubles, as a result of an unlucky forfeiting of self-respect, never understand what is happening to them until it is too late. The process is gradual, the danger invisible. But outsiders who know the facts can often see the poison working in the victim.

In the instance just cited, a large toll of happiness was taken by outraged self-respect as the result of a minor lapse, one condoned to some extent by the popular tradition of "finders keepers." Where the unlucky person has no social support whatever for his violation of self-respect, the penalty may be even more severe. The wise French proverb which says, "A successful stroke of dishonesty is the misfortune of many a good man," sums up an inescapable truth. The full extent of the misfortune is shown in the case of an unemployed young man to whom chance brought the offer of an attractive job—provided that he could meet all of the requirements. Some of these he lacked; it became plain that to get the job he would have to lie about some important aspects of his background.

When he decided to resist the temptation, he was astonished to have his father, whom he greatly admired, advise him to go after the job, lies or no lies. The arguments were, "You'll never have as good a chance again," and

"You have to make compromises to get on in this world." It never occurred to the young man that chronic financial worry might have corrupted his father's judgment. Impressed, he followed this unfortunate counsel.

The job was fairly well-paid, but its acceptance proved disastrous. The unlucky young man found himself trapped in a lie around which he had to build his whole life for the next twenty years. These years were marked by ceaseless anxiety, mounting personality troubles, weakness in all human relationships, and persistent misfortune—until finally, at the age of forty, unable to live with himself any longer, he committed suicide.

It is not an uncommon case. Modern psychologists say that a tendency to self-destruction is latent in everyone. With the loss of self-respect this tendency becomes active, and those who are conscious of despising themselves often turn to death as an escape from their thoughts. The words of W. H. Auden's "Prince Alpha" speak to the hearts of these unfortunates:

> Was I born, was it only to see
> I'm as tired of life as life of me?

Others reveal their misery unconsciously, often by a proneness to accidents. There are some people, physically healthy, who almost seem to make it a practice to slip in the bathtub, fall off ladders, and get in the way of motor-cars. In factories a very large proportion of accidents is often sustained by a small percentage of workmen who injure themselves time after time while the men around them, working at no less hazardous tasks, have little trouble. "The death wish," as psychoanalysis calls it, is certainly not the only reason for this condition; but evidence shows that in many cases the person who is hurt in one accident after another is not so much the victim of bitter chance as of a bitter heart.

THE ROLE OF CONSCIENCE IN LUCK

Curiously enough, in view of the facts of life, there are many who shrug at the word "self-respect," never realizing the effect of their attitude on their own luck. In their view, it is lucky to get money and enjoy yourself, self-respect or no. Their only test of luck is material success, even if it is criminal success. They fancy that they possess tough and realistic minds, and justify themselves by saying, like one of them, "What's the use of kidding ourselves? We live in a jungle world. Survival of the fittest is the law of life. The only way we get on is by tearing each other down. It is all right for the rich to talk about self-respect—they can afford the luxury of a conscience—but anybody who has ever experienced real poverty and has been kicked around all his life is not going to stop to think about self-respect if he can get hold of a million dollars without risk or if he can save his skin by telling a lie or if he finds a beautiful woman in his arms who has no business being there."

We cannot lightly dismiss this widespread feeling. Certainly, the temptation to transgress the social code under which we live is often very great, and becomes greater as the risk of being found out diminishes. Certainly, too, no normal person can go through life without a good many transgressions—especially when he has to struggle for the crumbs of life. But those who think that they can find luckiness at the expense of self-respect miss an essential point. It cannot be done. The psychology of today teaches that *the sense of right and wrong conditioned in us by our society—the "superego"—plays a vital part in keeping our minds healthy and stable.* Persistently ignore the superego, and remorse, like the deadly shirt of Nessus that killed Hercules, gradually envelops the transgressor, making him writhe with pain every moment of his way, driving him into unbalanced behavior that tempts misfortune. At root, the desire for self-respect, expressed in the protests of conscience, is evidence of the instinctive urge to live as a man among men, and not even the most cynical materialist can safely defy it.

We can, of course, point to crooks, hoodlums, and

grafters, and even to some buccaneers of legitimate business who have, to all appearances, killed self-respect and yet lived in physical comfort for long lifetimes. Leaving "ordinary people" to worry about right and wrong, they commit every crime from shoplifting to murder without remorse. Some might consider them lucky. Are they? Does their freedom from the usual taboos mean happiness for them? We are safe in asserting that it does not. Such men not only run obvious risks of reprisal by society, but in most cases, according to the available psychological evidence, they actually pay heavy penalties which do not necessarily appear on the surface of their lives. The stifling of conscience merely means that *the psychic trouble within them seeks other outlets*, such as the warping of the personality through neurotic fear or snarling cynicism.

Emotions like these, long sustained, destroy the capacity for love and friendship, isolate their victims from mankind, and generate a bitter sense of loneliness and insecurity which, as we have seen, invites bad luck. Many who practice piracy of one sort or another on their fellows often reveal painful psychic disturbance by middle age. They hunger for the affection or respect of others until the lack of it obsesses them and fills them with hatred. They have not escaped pain by killing conscience; they have only delayed it, and sharpened it. Instead of suffering self-reproach immediately following their misdeeds, and getting over it, they are likely to experience the prolonged misery which comes from overwhelming frustration of basic desires.

THE LUCKINESS OF SELF-RESPECT REAFFIRMED

On the brighter side of the coin, by maintaining self-respect men can extract good luck even from chances which, on the surface, are unfavorable. A dramatic illustration of the point is embodied in a newspaper story which appeared in the *New York World-Telegram* of February 3, 1942.

Lucky He Was Shot, Hero Says

Leonard Weisberg believes the luckiest moment in his life was when a bullet from the gun of one of the mad-dog Esposito brothers crashed into his throat, deflected from a collar bone, and landed at the base of his neck.

"It isn't a nice thought," the ex-cabbie, now a liquor store proprietor, said today, "but it led to something I've always wanted. . . ."

The 38-year-old hero of the gun battle on crowded Fifth Avenue a year ago . . . risked his own life in an attempt to save that of a friend, Patrolman Edward J. Maher. . . .

"I'd still be hacking if it hadn't happened," he said. "This way, with people kind and interested, I have a business of my own, and I'm getting somewhere in the community."

It was just a year ago today that Weisberg was released from a hospital after three weeks in which doctors despaired of his ability to speak again. After another week at home . . . he disposed of a new cab given him as a present. . . .

Weisberg invested the money from the cab sale in a liquor store. Knowing nothing of the business, he enlisted the aid of friends and put in stock and opened for business, the windows decorated with newspaper photographs and pictures of the Esposito shooting on January 14.

> "Business was good right from the start," he said. "People would drop in just to take a look at me, and then they would become regular customers. . . ."

This is obviously an exceptional case, remote, it may first appear, from our own problem of bringing luck into everyday pursuits. Actually, Weisberg's story reveals a basic pattern of good luck which has meaning for all of us. Quickly summarized, this pattern, like the formula for bad luck described earlier in this chapter, hinges on four points: (1) chance offers a compelling choice between a hazardous action which maintains self-respect and a safe one which weakens self-respect; (2) the individual concerned takes the risk in order to maintain self-respect; (3) he undergoes temporary loss or suffering; (4) he finds eventual compensations which more than offset his loss or suffering.

What are the compensations? No one, of course, can be sure that material rewards, like Weisberg's, will flow from actions taken to preserve self-respect. The real reward of such actions lies within: freedom from self-reproach—peace of mind. More than anything else, the intangible of inner tranquillity makes our self-respecting actions stand out as lucky milestones in life.

At the same time, there can be no doubt that self-respecting behavior frequently results in strong new luck-lines, over which material benefits flow. In a characteristic instance, an employee in a company learned that a co-worker was about to be fired for a mistake that she herself had made. Since the mistake was not traceable to her, she could have kept quiet, but self-respect drove her to prevent the injustice. Her confession brought about her own dismissal, but two days later the very man who had fired her called her up. The matter had been on his mind, he said. She had acted courageously, and he did not think she ought to be penalized. Although he could not rehire her, he knew of a job that was open in another concern, and he would be glad to recommend her. Within a week she had a job better than the one she had lost—together with her self-respect. But even without this immediate stroke of luck, her long-run prospects for a lucky life were infinitely greater than if she had crushed self-respect in order to cling to fancied economic security; for sooner or later the psychological consequences of that error would inevitably have caught up with her.

Experience shows that many people, while they recognize the potency of self-respect in the luck-process, feel uncomfortable about accepting all its implications. Even if we are willing to sacrifice money for self-respect, they ask, how far are we to carry this thesis? Are we to pretend to be heroes, risk our health, limbs, or life itself for self-respect?

Although the case of Weisberg, cited earlier, turned out luckily, are there not many more which end in hospitals, wheel chairs, and forgotten graves?

We cannot discuss this question without remembering the millions of soldiers and sailors who in wartime risk their lives as a matter of course. On the battlefield they are not infrequently faced with decisions which challenge self-respect—as when a comrade's life is at stake. If they make the self-respecting choice, it may be that they will end as forgotten heroes, unlucky victims of enemy guns. Would it not be better for them to "play it safe"?

Although it is easy to preach in these matters, and hard to practice, it must be said that the man, soldier or civilian, who would rather accept danger than inflict a permanent wound on his self-respect makes a wise choice. Any opportunity to reaffirm self-respect is in a sense a favorable chance, in spite of accompanying risks. There are times when any person of spirit has to say, with Ibsen's Dr. Stockman, "Who the devil cares whether there is risk or not? What I am doing, I am doing in the name of truth and for my own conscience."

Few are called upon to be heroes, or to perform spectacular actions. For most of us the obligation is only to try to maintain self-respect in the chances of everyday life. That is where violations of self-respect show their grimmest consequences. The man who, rather than take a risk, lets others suffer when he could save them—the man who consistently betrays his faith, his convictions, or his friends before he will risk personal inconvenience—such a man, even if he should prosper materially, can scarcely avoid paying the terrible penalty of the unlucky in neurotic and even psychotic disturbances.

IT IS NEVER TOO LATE
TO REAFFIRM SELF-RESPECT

Fortunately for most of us, the occasional violence we do our self-respect is only occasional. Self-respect resists destruction; even when it droops, if given a little encouragement, a little protection against blight, it will raise its head and thrive again. However we may have transgressed in the past, we all have the power to reinvigorate our self-respect and to rise by degrees above weakening remorse and self-reproach. By availing ourselves of chances to reaffirm self-respect, we build up our luck-potential as by no other means. Even persons so far gone in cynicism and self-hatred that there seemed no hope for them have found new self-respect within themselves, and by conscious effort rejoined the company of well-adjusted, life-loving, lucky men and women.

A single self-respecting action, taken when the personality was in danger of becoming permanently enfeebled, can perform a miracle of regeneration. Many a man, looking back over his life, sees as its luckiest moment the occasion when chance permitted him to confess a wrong that he had concealed, to restore something that was not his to the rightful owner, to admit a lie or correct a false impression, to accept responsibility for a problem of his own making, to give up an unfair advantage over another, to stand up manfully against injustice, or to protect someone too weak to protect himself. It is through such actions that we sharply raise our luck-potential, enormously strengthening our power to distinguish between lucky and unlucky chances for the rest of our lives.

The way in which chance uses self-respect as a bridge to the full development of a human being shows itself dramatically in a story from the life of one of the world's great men, Mahatma Gandhi. The year was 1892. Gandhi was twenty-three years of age, and had recently become a lawyer. Deeply affected by Western ideas, he was intensely ambitious for personal success. At the time he was practicing law in the little principality of Porbandar, where he was dependent for cases on the resident British agent. This official made no secret of his contempt for Indians, but Gandhi cultivated him, nevertheless, in the hope of advancement.

One day when Gandhi called at the agent's office to discuss some matter, he found the man in a furious temper, and when he attempted to speak, was forcibly ejected. The shock of this chance, as Gandhi put it, "changed the course of my entire life." Self-respect was challenged. A lesser man might have tried to make his peace with the agent, but Gandhi sensed the danger of undermining his character by sycophancy. Rather than run such a risk, he gave up his law practice and family ties in Porbandar, and decided, in his own words, "to try my luck in South Africa," where there was a large Hindu community.

On his first day in the new continent he bought a first-class ticket on the train that was to carry him to Capetown. Soon after the train started, however, a guard forced him out of his compartment on the ground that only white men were permitted to travel first class. The fact that he had been sold a first-class ticket made no difference.

It was then night, and the train had stopped at the town of Maritzburg, in Natal. Gandhi refused to enter a second-class carriage; instead he got off the train. All night long he sat in the cold station, and sought guidance. This experience, he said later, was the most creative in his life. He saw only one course open to him—to follow the line of self-respect. At dawn he bought another first-class ticket to Capetown; and when the train arrived, he entered a first-class carriage. In it he found an Englishman, who ignored him. Presently the compartment door opened, and an incensed guard ordered Gandhi to leave. When he protested, the guard threatened violence; but at this moment the Englishman intervened, and ordered the guard to leave Gandhi alone.

The encouraging discovery that not all Englishmen were slaves to race prejudice was the one thing that was needed to show Gandhi his future course. For the next twenty years, invoking help from fair-minded and democratic Englishmen, he fought a battle for the civil rights of Indians in South Africa. He won; and the spiritual discoveries made in the course of this experience enabled him to return to India and lead her subsequent struggle for independence. The preservation of his self-respect under the pressure of chance brought luck at the highest level, not only into his life, but into the life of a great nation.

DON'T CONFUSE SELF-RESPECT WITH PRIDE

At this point, a warning should be posted. It is easy to confuse self-respect with pride—and pride, far from being lucky, is a positively unlucky trait. "No man ever had a point of pride that was not injurious to him," wrote Edmund Burke. To resist this truth is to hamper oneself throughout life. *However noble a mask pride may wear, we cannot afford to let it dictate decisions affecting our luck.*

In contrast to self-respect, pride—whether it be of origin, beauty, position, achievement, or anything else—is fundamentally an expression of insecurity, with its roots in illusion. It is a sign that the individual is trying to cover up a feeling of spiritual weakness by pointing to some superficial advantage or external superiority. The danger to luck is revealed in a thousand ways. There are, for example, many who take excessive risks merely to show off their strength, bravery, or skill; tempted by pride, they stake far more than they stand to gain on a fling of fortune. Then, too, we have those other proud persons, insecure at heart, who are unable to accept justifiable reprimands or criticism—who quit jobs and leave homes and walk out of meetings at the slightest affront. Such people are natural targets for bad luck; thinking that they are maintaining self-respect when they are only indulging pride, they cannot clearly estimate the risks they take.

A case in point is that of a young Frenchman who occupied a position of consequence in France's Ministry of Foreign Affairs, at a time of great political tension. One day he took two ladies to lunch at a crowded restaurant, where they were wretchedly served by a surly waiter.

When presently they had to leave to keep an engagement, they had been given only a part of the meal they had ordered. Unable to find the waiter, or to catch the eye of the maître d'hôtel, the official, in hot anger, tossed on the table enough money to pay for the food consumed, but none to pay for the ordered food yet to come or for the tip. Then he and his companions left the restaurant.

They hailed a taxi, but had hardly seated themselves when the waiter rushed out, hurling noisy insults at the official. The taxi driver, delighted with the scene, kept his cab at the curb, forcing the official to make a difficult decision: should he compel the waiter to apologize or should he try to pass the incident off without a public scandal? At once his mind foresaw the possibility of a street brawl, a policeman, a newspaper report, and a source of new attacks on the government.

The ladies urged him to ignore the cursing waiter. Outraged pride, however, won the day. He had been "insulted." Leaving the cab, he satisfied his ego by punching the waiter, who fought back. A few minutes later, the official found himself compelled to give his name to an *agent de police* who was entirely indifferent to his high rank. All the unlucky consequences that he had foreseen soon developed—newspaper stories, malicious cartoons, an attack on him in the Chamber of Deputies, and finally, so much embarrassment for his Minister that the young man felt obliged to resign.

Here was an instance of unlucky confusion between pride—which put the claim of the ego above responsibility to others—and self-respect. It was easy for him to fight with the waiter, who incidentally also had some cause for anger. It would have been harder, but far luckier, for the official to accept the slight to pride, and let self-respect dictate his appraisal of the chance. For example, he might have returned to the restaurant, explained his position fully to the waiter and the proprietor, and made sure that neither had been defrauded. In this way, he might have had to swallow rancor, but he would have protected his government, the dignity of his companions, and his own luck.

The measure of a man's self-respect, far from being his pride, is more likely to be the extent to which he is willing to subdue pride in a good cause. The case of a man who, during the depression of the 1930's, held on for years to a frustrating job under a sadistic boss is characteristic. No hour passed when he did not want to resign—but he and his family were desperately poor; he had little chance of getting another job; he could not sacrifice his wife and children to his own feelings. The ordeal was long and painful, and yet he emerged from it unscathed.

His pride had suffered, true, but not his self-respect. By swallowing the attacks on his ego, in a cause bigger than himself, he had maintained his self-respect and his luck-potential—as he could never have done if, out of pride, he had submitted his family to great distress. It is when we sharply separate self-respect from pride and vanity that it serves us best as a guide in the selection and rejection of chances.

6

THE INTUITIVE APPROACH TO LUCK

"For we know in part, and we prophesy in part."

CORINTHIANS

I don't know why, but I feel that—" is a phrase that, properly understood, has enormous power to bring us good luck. The role of intuition in the luck-process is to question or reinforce judgment; it often reveals in a flash more than we could figure out in a lifetime. Below the threshold of consciousness is a kind of secret reference library of unspoken knowledge and forgotten impressions, and the unconscious mind at certain times will pull out the evidence that bears on the risk before one, delivering its verdict in the mysterious form of intuition.

People of a highly practical turn of mind, who refuse to accept any phenomenon that they cannot explain in detail, sometimes tend to sneer at intuition because its processes are obscure. It is true that intuition, as a concept, does easily slide into considerations of extrasensory perception, telepathy, and clairvoyance—an area of human experience as yet full of darkness and fantasy. In the normal business of life, however, the workings of intuition are sufficiently evident so that anyone who discounts its importance runs the danger of losing the aid of one of man's most useful allies in appraising the chances of life. The poet who called intuition "the crown of reason" spoke a truth which commands our attention.

LUCKY PEOPLE, LUCKY DAYS

Poets, composers, scientists, and creative people of all kinds usually learn to depend heavily on their intuitive perceptions. Thus, the great mathematician Gauss wrote of one of his discoveries: "At last I succeeded, not by painful effort, but so to speak by the grace of God. As a sudden flash of truth the enigma was solved. For my part I am not in a position to point to the thread which joins what I knew previously to what I have succeeded in doing."

He was only one of many who have recorded similar experiences. For most of us, however, perhaps the essential function of intuition in the luck-process is less spectacular, if equally valuable. It lies in providing quick estimates of people. The nonintuitive person, encountering a stranger, will either have no opinion about him or will base his opinion on observed and usually superficial aspects of appearance and behavior. The intuitive person, on the other hand, is likely to have a feeling rather than an opinion: like or dislike, trust or distrust, approval or disapproval, and this feeling can seldom be accounted for in so many words.

Our intuitive judgments of others may sometimes arise from unconscious impressions of previous experiences with people of similar characteristics. But in many instances they are more complex than that. A wife has been known to say to her husband, of a new friend, "I hope you do not see much of him. I have the feeling that he is unlucky for you." The husband scoffed at what he considered nonsense, but the friendship later led to serious business troubles, which caused him much suffering. Telling of this incident, he said, "Jim (the friend) was a good fellow, but I felt highly competitive toward him. He brought out the worst in me."

It is a familiar complaint. No one can afford to forget that while he is influencing other people, they are also influencing him, for better or for worse. Another personality, merely by being what it is, can push us to respond to chance at the top level of our potential behavior, or at the bottom. It can bring out the worst or the best in us, depending on the way in which its characteristics excite our own. In the presence of a man of great integrity and nobility of spirit, we are likely to feel exalted; whereas those who make us feel competitive easily can tempt us into unlucky displays of egoism. Obviously, if there are many people whose personalities tend to bring out the worst in us, we need to examine our own psychological state with great care, for in this situation there is a distinct hint of dangerous weakness. The essential point, however, is that *intuition can help us recognize that another person is lucky or unlucky for us.*

So, too, intuition can sometimes tell us how a certain period of time stands in relation to our luck. The lucky or unlucky day is no mere illusion, for the fluctuations in our energy-state can have a great deal to do with our ability to recognize and respond to chance. We all have days when nothing goes well and when bad luck seems to hover in the air around us. It is not at all superstitious to take such feelings seriously. When we sense an unfavorable condition in ourselves, we do well to proceed with utmost caution in all of our judgments and enterprises.

Little mishaps in home or office have many times been preludes to larger misfortunes. This is certainly not to say that we should seek for omens. To attribute magical power to things seen or done by chance is, as we shall see presently, not only irrational but fundamentally unlucky. But there is nothing superstitious about recognizing the implications of our unconscious actions. Dr. Sigmund Freud is among the many psychologists who have stressed this point. "The Roman who . . . withdrew from an undertaking because he had stumbled on his threshold . . . was a better psychologist than we . . . ," he wrote. "For his stumbling could demonstrate to him the existence of a doubt . . . the force of which could weaken the power of his intention at the moment of its execution. For only by concentrating all psychic forces on the desired aim can one be assured of success."

Our inadvertent behavior can be a significant clue to our fitness, at a given time, to respond to a chance that may seriously affect our luck. To accept such guidance from the unconscious mind is entirely reasonable. Similarly, we are wise to let intuition speak to us when we face chance situations which require us to make decisions. Many a man has saved himself from peril when intuition told him to select this day rather than that, this hour, and not another, for some crucial action. The mysterious sense of timing that has helped so many great political, military, and business leaders to rise to power—Franklin D. Roosevelt, Eisenhower, Bernard Baruch—is largely a matter of intuition.

But here the fact must be faced that intuitions can easily be counterfeited. While the genuine intuition is a force for good luck, nothing is more fatal to our fortunes than the spurious hunch. To imagine and invent intuitions is to put judgment into a strait jacket. When people move constantly in a fog of self-deception about their intuitions—and many do—they are almost sure to mistake some will-o'-the-wisp of chance for a guiding light, until it leads them over the brink of misfortune.

DISTINGUISHING INTUITIONS FROM WISHES

The false and unlucky intuition usually results from confusion between the workings of the unconscious mind and our conscious wishes, fears, and superstitions. It is important to see clearly the nature of this danger. Consider, for example, the menace of the wish-hunch. In one case a girl told her mother, "I realize John is a heavy drinker, but I just know I can make him stop drinking after we get married. I feel absolutely convinced of it." Intuition? She thought so. But two years later, when she was obtaining her divorce, she bitterly confessed to her mother, "I always was afraid he would never stop drinking. But I was in love with him, and I had to think I could help him." By mistaking a wish for an intuition, and allowing it to overrule her judgment, this girl underestimated the risk of the chance she was taking. *Apparent intuitions which coincide with strong wishes and which involve high risks should always be regarded with suspicion.*

Two insidious forms of the wish-hunch are especially

common. One is the feeling that we are somehow bound to be luckier than the next fellow, no matter what we do. This feeling can lead to conduct so irrational as almost to defy belief. For example, psychologists at a Western university examined certain nickel slot machines which were patronized extensively by the students. It was discovered that the chance of winning the jack pot, which amounted to five dollars, was only one in about a thousand. The facts were disclosed to the students. A month later a check-up was made to discover how many of them were still gambling with the machines. Eighty per cent were still playing. On questioning, 35 per cent said that they "had a hunch" they were going to win the jack pot.

A second type of unlucky wish-hunch often comes in the form of the dream in which we fulfill some desire. The dream is harmless enough; the bad luck arises when the dreamer makes the mistake of allowing the wish expressed in the dream to substitute for a genuine intuition. To be sure, dreams do occasionally come true, but to translate dream-wishes into action, against our conscious judgment of the risk, is to beg for a blow from fortune. A French soldier in World War I, Capt. Alain Jolivet, has told amusingly the result of one such wish-hunch. In his vivid dream he saw himself in a certain nearby French village, then reputed to be in German hands. The village was deserted, and he fortified it in time to help smash a great German offensive. The commander in chief then congratulated him for his foresight and recommended him for the *Croix de Guerre* and a promotion. Jolivet awoke all excited from this pleasant dream, took a few picked men, and cautiously headed for the village. At the outskirts they were met by a strong German patrol which fired on them and took them prisoners. Jolivet was wounded, and spent the next two years in a prison camp.

WHEN ARE PREMONITIONS RELIABLE?

Occasionally the dream does bring a genuine intuition to the surface; the philosopher Descartes, for example, heard certain words spoken in a dream, and those words became the core of his entire philosophy. It is rare, however, for the unconscious to use the dream form in order to provide a direct guidance in the chances of life. More frequently the dream produces intuitions of a premonitory kind: "By a divine instinct men's minds mistrust ensuing dangers." There is no doubt that many people have found in dreams warnings of things to come, which their unconscious minds perceived long before their consciousness. But *unless experience has taught us to rely on our dream-premonitions, it is wise to regard them with a degree of skepticism.* Psychoanalysts teach that the dream is often the expression of a hidden conflict between reason and instinct, and to unravel its involved symbolism requires much more self-knowledge than most of us have.

The premonitions of our waking hours are likely to be far more important to our luck than those of sleep. Many people have had unaccountable anticipations of danger that put them on their guard and saved their lives. A man walking on a country road in a pitch black night has been known to stop with a sudden sense of uneasiness and strike a light, which revealed a coiled copperhead a few paces ahead of him. Had he heard the snake move or hiss? Not that he knew. To him, it seemed only that some unseen force had pulled him back from the deadly menace that would have been under his feet in three more steps.

No doubt some "true" premonitions, whether born in dreams or in waking, are no more than coincidences between neurotic fears and the play of chance. The point is illustrated in a childhood luck-story related by the late David Belasco, the well-known theatrical producer. A boat excursion had been planned for the children of his neighborhood; he was all eagerness to go, and his mother had agreed. When he went aboard the waiting steamer, however, he saw her crying on the dock. He knew that she always worried about him, frequently to the point of tears, but impulsively he rushed down the gangplank and stood at her side, watching the boat leave without him. A few hours later they heard that a frightful explosion had destroyed the boat, taking a tragic toll of life.

Memorable though the incident was for Belasco, it can scarcely be regarded as more than a striking coincidence. Similar cases, where the persistent anxiety feelings of a doting mother coincide with an occasional accident, are not uncommon. Many people have fears of accident which are quickly forgotten except in those rare instances when they happen to come true. It is hardly necessary to add that intuitions growing out of neurotic anxiety are not likely to be a reliable guide in most chance situations.

DISTINGUISHING BETWEEN
SUPERSTITION AND INTUITION

Most common, most painful, and unluckiest of the errors made about intuition is its confusion with superstition. At horse races people who rely on omens are the favorite prey of the bookmaker. Successful gamblers may have pet superstitions—but they do not rely on them when taking big risks. Their point of view is usually that of John W. (Bet-a-million) Gates, who once said mockingly to a questioner, "Sure, I'm superstitious. I never bet on a horse numbered seven unless I'm pretty sure it will win."

Not only in gambling but in all the chances of life,

superstition invites bad luck by causing us to underestimate real risks. A classic example was reported in 1940 by a New York City social worker. It is the case of a married man "on relief" who, although out of a job, insisted on taking into his home the two babies of an unemployed friend whose wife had died. "My Maria will look after them together with our own kids," he said, and his hard-working wife loyally did her best to live up to his expectations.

Shortly afterward the husband got a good job. "See," he told his wife, "those kids of Tony's have brought us luck." Timidly she suggested that they send the babies back to Tony, who had also found a job—especially as there was so much cooking and washing and nursing to do for their own three children. Her husband was indignant at the suggestion. Generosity was no longer in question, but superstition was. "I tell you Tony's kids have brought us luck," he insisted. "We'll keep them as long as Tony doesn't ask for them back."

A month later his wife collapsed from overwork and was taken to the hospital for a long and expensive stay. The husband, deeply shocked, had to return Tony's children in spite of himself. This was his comment: "Well, of course we had bad luck. That's because Maria wanted to send the kids back home. She spoiled our luck."

A "lucky" stroke of superstition can be a calamity if it

causes the victim to lean on a hollow belief and to under-estimate the risks of chances that come his way. To in-dulge a primitive belief in magic is to hold out our necks for the ax of chance. Yet many do precisely that. The number of persons, adults as well as children, who rely on superstition startles the investigator. Sometimes the very people who deny in words that they are superstitious seek for omens and portents at every turn, secretly feel that if they can only find the right talisman all will go well for them, and blame their bad luck on evil conjunctions of the stars.

HARMLESS AND HARMFUL SUPERSTITION

All this does not mean that the holding of a superstition is necessarily unlucky. Not a bit of it. A deeply buried im-pulse to superstition, inherited from our prehistoric past, is in all of us. Unless we sometimes satisfy this impulse, it may disturb us by giving us vague, unreasonable feelings of insecurity or doubt. For example, there is nothing in the least foolish in thinking that a favorite color on the walls of the room in which we work can be lucky for us; through its influence on our unconscious mind it can help us to relax, feel stronger and more secure. A "lucky num-ber" on our automobile license plate can have a similar beneficial effect in aiding our unconscious to combat anxieties which tend to destroy concentration and invite accidents.

Similarly, a superstitious gesture, even if we do not take it seriously, can occasionally bolster our confidence and that of our associates. The late Mayor of New York City, Fiorello LaGuardia, for example, had a favorite campaign superstition. When a new election approached, he brought out an ancient black overcoat which he had had since 1919, and which he called his "lucky coat." Toward the close of the campaign he would put on the coat and make a trip uptown to his "lucky" corner—the intersection of 116th Street and Lexington Avenue in Harlem. A small crowd would gather, he would deliver a short speech, and then he would go home, feeling relaxed and confident. But it is obvious that LaGuardia did not rely on superstition for his confidence. At no point did it interfere with his careful preparation and hard work. He indulged his superstition because he knew that it had a certain psychological value for him and his supporters.

Many exceptionally able men, like LaGuardia, have a lucky talisman. With Franklin D. Roosevelt, a hat served the purpose—a weather-beaten gray fedora which he wore through his first three Presidential campaigns. After the third, on November 4, 1940, when he believed that he would never be a candidate again, he contributed the hat to an auction for the benefit of the Motion Picture

Relief Fund, reputedly causing Mrs. Roosevelt to remark with amusement, "I thought he would never part with it. He is very superstitious about that hat." At the auction the hat was bought, against stiff competition, by the noted actors Edward G. Robinson and Melvyn Douglas, who kept it until 1944, when the President decided to run once more for re-election. Its return to him at that time gave the President much pleasure, and he wore it on his successful campaign tour. Today it reposes, symbol of a friendly and harmless superstition, in the Franklin D. Roosevelt Library at Hyde Park, New York.

Any little superstition that we may practice to increase our confidence in moments of crisis is harmless, and may even be helpful, so long as we do not rely on it. As soon as we *do* rely on it, however, bad luck peeps around the corner. Some years ago the young daughter of a wealthy family suddenly disappeared after a visit to New York City. Her distressed parents spent weeks of anguish until she finally was found by detectives in a cheap lodging-house in Hollywood. Under questioning she showed them a stick of grease paint which she said she had received from the brilliant actress Helen Hayes during a visit to the star's dressing room after a theatrical performance. With this luck charm she felt confident that she too could become a famous actress, so she immediately took herself to California in the hope of achieving an overnight success in motion pictures. But after visiting a few studios and casting offices she had been so discouraged that she had given up all hope. Only pride had prevented her from returning home.

It is when superstition masquerades as intuition that it carries especial danger of bad luck. Mayor LaGuardia's coat and this girl's stick of grease paint were both fetishes, but the girl relied on her fetish alone, and it caused her to underestimate the risk she took.

THREE QUESTIONS ABOUT YOUR INTUITION

The luck-value of intuition, clearly distinguished from wishes, fears, and superstitions, is plain enough. How intuition can be consciously used to improve our luck, however, may not at once be so clear. Certainly, we cannot hope to produce intuitions to order every time we are confronted by a knotty chance. The intuitive approach to luck really lies in our ability to answer three questions which bear directly on the way in which we appraise life's chances.

The first of these questions is: *Am I an intuitive person?* There are, of course, great differences in the frequency of intuitions, as between one person and another. People of a strongly logical turn of mind seem on the whole to be less intuitive than persons who rely little on logic, but whose senses are highly developed. There can hardly be any doubt that women are on the whole more intuitive than men, especially in the area of human relations, although some men are remarkable for the frequency and validity of their intuitive judgments of other people. Generally speaking, it appears that most people are more intuitive than they realize. Intuitions are often so quickly backed up or pushed aside by reason that we are hardly aware of them. We sense intuitively that a man is unreliable, but immediately our conscious mind offers us reasons for the conviction, and the reasons monopolize our attention. Usually we remember our intuitions only when we cannot discern a factual foundation for them and when they nevertheless prove to be true. There may be many others which play a useful part in helping us to appraise chances but which slip quickly out of memory.

But don't overestimate the power of intuition because it has proved accurate in a single instance. There should be repeated evidence of the reliability of one's intuition before heavy weight is put on it in the appraisal of risks. *If we are strongly intuitive, we can usually find a good deal of specific evidence of the fact in our experience.* In evaluating that experience, it is, of course, important to be honest with ourselves. One not infrequently meets a woman who prides herself on her intuitive judgments of people whom she meets for the first time, but who on better acquaintance usually revises her opinions of them, conveniently forgetting her original hunches. If she persists in sanctifying her intuitions and regarding them as a safe guide in the chances of life, she can hardly avoid a good deal of bad luck.

The way an intuition expresses itself may be a clue to its validity. If it is strong and persistent, it is likely to be far more trustworthy than if it flits quickly in and out of the mind. For example, a stock market specialist, noted for his luck, says that about nine times out of ten his hunches regarding price movements are no better than anybody else's, but that the tenth time it is as if an alarm clock had gone off in his unconscious mind, and on these occasions he has never been wrong. Accordingly, he makes it a point never to let a hunch dictate his estimate of a risk "unless the alarm clock rings."

Our second question about intuition, the answer to which may strongly influence our luck, is: *In what areas of life am I most intuitive?* While we may be highly intuitive in some fields, in others our unconscious mind may give us no aid whatever. Some scientists, intuitive where their work is concerned, are entirely dependent on conscious observation and thought in their estimates of people. Dowsers and well-diggers often "feel in their bones" the presence of underground water, but may utterly lack intuition in business matters. A physician with acute intuitions of personal character, when persuaded to run for political office, showed himself unable to sense the feelings of crowds. We need to review our own experience of intuition to determine the areas in which our unconscious may be relied on to identify favorable chances.

Finally, this question demands consideration: *Under what conditions am I most intuitive?* Here again there is wide variation. Some people are more intuitive in the presence of others than they are alone. One man's intuitive powers respond immediately to new surroundings; whereas another's will manifest themselves only after an interval of time.

Many creative workers have found that they can deliberately invite intuitions by closing their eyes and relaxing their bodies. We associate the closing of the eyes with sleep, and our unconscious impulses and feelings always seem closer to the surface in the dark. If the unconscious has an intuition for us, it has a better chance of coming across the borderline of consciousness when we are relaxed. Men in the professions and in business will frequently keep notebooks at their bedside in order to jot down such borderline thoughts before they are forgotten.

But rest is not the only good incubator for intuitions. Mozart, for example, found that musical themes came to him most readily when he played billiards, while Haydn received his greatest inspirations during solitary prayer, and the astronomer Sir William Hamilton discovered that long walks encouraged his intuitive perceptions. *At times when we seek ideas or are confronted by risk, it is wise to expose ourselves so far as we can to conditions under which we are most likely to be intuitive, with past experience as our guide.*

Careful observation of our total experience with the crown of reason over a period of time can be of great value in luck-development. Sound intuitions are a form of insurance against defects in conscious judgment. Face to face with risk, the intuitive person has a far better chance of being lucky than one who has to rely entirely on calculation. The conscious test of any chance, as we have seen, requires us to determine whether it accords with our real desires, our real abilities, our considered judgment, and our self-respect. To these important determinations, we now need to add another question: *What is my intuitive feeling about the chance—and is it free from wishful thinking, the contamination of fear, and superstition?* Only the chance that accords with desires, abilities, judgment, and self-respect, and that does not run counter to a strong and honest intuition, carries the promise of luck.

PART THREE

The Response to Chance

1

THE POWER OF THE RESPONSE

"What have you, my good friends,
deserved at the hands of fortune?"

SHAKESPEARE

As we noted in the Opening Statement, there is a kind of ready-made luck, like a fatal accident, that leaves us no room for response. Men whose occupations demand that they hazard their lives—soldiers, sailors, test-pilots, deep-sea divers—usually think of their luck as beyond their power to affect, and so it may be, as it relates to the stray bullet, the sinking ship, the missing engine, the broken cable. Perhaps, too, we may speak of the ready-made luck of birth; for the uniting of certain genes and chromosomes to produce a baby of specific characteristics, the circumstances of his birth, and the conditions into which he is born are surely among the major chances of existence.

Once that is said, however, the vast realm of luck that remains is seen to be ruled, not by chance alone, but jointly, by chance and by ourselves. After childhood the great majority of life's chances demand a definite response from us before they fully reveal their luck-content. *And the nature of the response can sharply alter the original tenor and trend of the chance.* It can extract misfortune from the most promising situations, or turn unfavorable chances into magnificent luck.

A case in point is that of the Irish Sweepstakes winner who, in the flush of his triumph, gave up his job and thereafter frittered away the prize money in a few months of extravagant living and foolish speculation. Broke, jobless, and embittered, he wound up much worse off than if he had never held the winning ticket. Here a sensational piece of ready-made good luck was converted by an unsound response into misfortune. The principle holds good throughout life. As the sculptor Rodin said, "Each of us carves his destiny in the raw clay of chance." If our feelings of insecurity and uncontrolled emotions prevent our responding effectively, the favoring chance itself can seldom save us from bad luck.

Not even high intelligence is enough to assure lucky responses unless it is grounded in firm character. In one instance, a young man of exceptional brain power and ability met a girl of noted and wealthy family under romantic circumstances. They were instantly attracted to each other; and to impress her, he embroidered his family background so that it would seem to be more nearly on a par with her own, when in fact it was entirely ordinary. Unfortunately, this man, for all his intelligence and education, had not grasped a fundamental axiom of psychology—that anyone who breaks with the absolute truth about himself sooner or later suffers a penalty, perhaps only in the invisible precincts of the mind, but real nevertheless.

In order to maintain the friendship he persisted in the lie, which he was forced to introduce into all his social contacts. Presently the truth emerged, to his embarrassment and pain. The girl, who loved him and who would not have let a question of social position stand in the way of their marriage, broke off the friendship. The respect which the young man lost among other people who knew him damaged his subsequent career as it had already damaged his moral fiber. He never really understood what had happened to him. Bitterness, resentment, and pessimism gripped him. Regarding himself as the victim of "bad breaks," he did not perceive the extent to which his own feelings of insecurity, expressed in his conscious choice of response, had combined with chance to produce his misfortune.

FROM MISCHANCE TO HAPPINESS

On the other hand, a seeming disaster can frequently be converted by sound response into an important stroke of good luck. I know a woman who considers an event of absolute horror one of the luckiest moments of her life. She was pregnant at the time, and was walking down a New York street when a suicide jumped out of a sky-scraper window, landing almost at her feet. She fainted at the terrible spectacle and was rushed to a hospital. Her chief fear on recovering from the shock was that through prenatal influence the incident might adversely affect her expected child. Doctors reassured her, but she was dis-satisfied. Determined to try to prevent such a calamity, she responded to this stroke of ready-made bad luck by mak-ing an intensive study of prenatal influence. The reading of every available book and article on the subject not only convinced her that she had nothing to fear, but more, it led her to an understanding of biology and infant psychol-ogy. As a result, she came out of this experience qualified to be a far better mother than she could have been without it; and her child, as he grew, showed great benefits from her insights into his problems. It is hardly surprising that she should have regarded this episode as lucky, for all its ugly beginnings.

Shock and pain, through a strong and constructive response, often open the mind more widely to life. Even diseases and ailments of the body are not necessarily unlucky. One example is a man who regards a peptic ulcer that once afflicted him as "a piece of luck." When it first troubled him, he was astonished to hear from his doctor that often such ills as ulcers, chronic constipation, insomnia, obesity, chronic headaches, premature hypertension and heart trouble can be traced to a wrong way of reacting to the circumstances of life, and cured more readily by psychotherapy than by medicine. After long resistance to the idea, he put himself in the hands of a psychiatrist. The healing of his ulcer was one result, but his greatest benefit was recognition of much that had been wrong with his attitude toward his environment. The enhanced satisfaction in living that he gained from this experience outweighed the pain he had suffered, and he was quite right in regarding this as a lucky passage of his life. Again it resulted, not from the chance alone, but from the interplay between chance and response.

We have all heard of people who have been crippled, blinded, or scarred and who, by responding to the tragic chance of their affliction with hope and energy, instead of despair, have surprised themselves by the amount of happy living still possible to them. Although in most cases they would hardly consider their trouble as having brought them good luck, they have nevertheless greatly mitigated their misfortune through their response. We cannot appraise the luck of our lives over any extended period without becoming aware of the way in which strokes of ready-made luck, as we respond to them, lose their original character and merge into the total stream of our fortunes.

Sometimes the lucky response may not even require energetic effort. A mere change of mind, from a psychologically insecure to a secure position or from selfishness to generosity, may be enough to produce a lucky result from an unfavorable chance. Such was the experience of George Bernard Shaw when, as a man of forty, he found good luck in a broken leg. He was at the time undecided whether to maintain his bachelor's freedom or to marry an amiable and wealthy young woman, Miss Charlotte Payne-Townshend, who, he knew, wanted to be his wife. Although he liked and respected her, he was not in love in any accepted sense of the phrase, and with his detached intellectualism, middle-aged habits, and resentment of intrusion on his privacy, he felt that the risks of unhappiness in marriage, any marriage, would be very great. He visited Miss Payne-Townshend at her country home and communicated these views to her, with considerable firmness.

Uneasy in the knowledge that he had caused the young lady pain, he was cycling back to the inn where he was staying when his bicycle hit an unseen rock and he fell heavily, breaking his leg. The news soon reached Miss Payne-Townshend. At once she sent word to Shaw, suggesting that he be brought from the inn to her house, where he could receive better care. The playwright had no illusions as to the obligation that he would contract if he accepted this invitation. Expediency alone would not have been enough to make him accept it. In this instance, chance and his own generous impulse pointed in the same direction; and for the next month Miss Payne-Townshend was his nurse, secretary, and companion. Their marriage, following as a natural sequel, brought into Shaw's life a mutuality of devotion and a stability that contributed much to his work and happiness.

WHAT MAKES A RESPONSE LUCKY?

As soon as we recognize the power of the response in determining our luck, the question arises: Why do some people respond to chance more successfully than others? What are the specific factors that condition their responses, and bring luck to them, whereas other men, just as eager for happiness, are snowed under by misfortune? We can answer this question with some certainty, for the facts become clear as soon as we examine the case histories of luck. The unavoidable conclusion is this: Underlying the sound responses of lucky people to chance are three predominant elements of their natures: *high energy, vigorous imagination, and strong faith*. More than any other characteristics, it is these "big three" personality traits that transform raw chance into good fortune.

But suppose we lack one or more of these qualities? Suppose we just happen to be lazy, unimaginative, or cynical by nature? Does that defect condemn us to bad luck? The question deserves a candid answer. There are some people, grossly deficient in most of the lucky attributes, who lack the will to struggle and so are unable ever to escape from the blows of life. Fortunately, they are a small minority. Most of us possess to a reasonable degree the three essential elements for lucky responses to chance. Or, if we are somewhat lacking in one or two of them, we are willing to try to do something about it.

That willingness is the gateway to better luck. A vigorous effort to develop ourselves in any lucky direction—and the effort is not nearly so hard as many who have never tried it believe—can go far to bring us into closer harmony with chance.

2

HOW INCREASED ENERGY
PRODUCES LUCK

*"With a twofold vigour lift me up to
reach at victory above my head."*

SHAKESPEARE

Here is a statement so obvious that one may easily lose sight of its great significance: *Much of our greatest luck comes to us when our energy is high.* The reason is shown in a story told by a businesswoman who was considering a contract to merge her small concern with another, larger firm. The document came to her in the mail late one afternoon, after an arduous day. As she read it, one clause in it struck her as being so grossly unfair to her that she indignantly decided that an attempt was being made to defraud her. At once she dictated a hot and angry letter, but as she signed it, preparatory to returning the contract, it occurred to her that it might be best to study the document again—perhaps she had missed some other point.

Too tired to tackle the job at the moment, she went home to dinner, and later, after she was fed and rested, opened her briefcase. This time, as she read the exasperating clause, it suddenly dawned on her that the one-sided wording that had aroused her anger might not have been deliberate; it might have been caused by the omission of a line by the typist. The next day at the office she destroyed her truculent letter and returned the unsigned contract with a courteous note calling attention to the presumptive omission. In reply she received a corrected contract and a good-humored apology, in which it was made clear that the error had been inadvertent. The letter went on to congratulate her on her powers of observation, and the episode, by creating a pleasant atmosphere around the negotiation, put her in an advantageous position.

The essential point of this story lies in the important role played by energy of response. In the first reading of the contract, the woman's mind was fatigued and stale, and as a result her response to the chance of the omitted line was hasty and ill-advised. Had she carried out her first intention, and so lost the opportunity of the merger, she would undoubtedly have regarded herself in the upshot as having had bad luck.

Heightened energy manifests itself in a number of specifically lucky ways—sometimes in a display of muscular power to meet a sudden chance, more frequently in the state of mind. Notably, three psychological attitudes, closely linked to energy, are of utmost importance to our luck: *presence of mind, confidence, and determination.* Their relation to the luck-process, and the ways in which they can best be developed, are what we must now examine.

THE LUCK-POWER OF PRESENCE OF MIND

We have already noted the part played by alertness in helping us to recognize lucky chances. As soon as we have identified the chance, the alert condition undergoes a profound change. We no longer watch concentratedly for something to happen. It has happened. Our problem now is to respond to it. Instead of keeping attention focused entirely on the chance event, we survey our surroundings—we "get the picture"—we see what things or circumstances near us can be of use in responding to the chance. It is in this survey that the quality called presence of mind shows its luck-power. The more accurate our picture of the situation is—the more clearly we see the relationship between its various elements—the more "present" our mind is, and the more likely we are to respond luckily to the chance.

Let us look at an actual example—an experience which befell the late Henry P. Davison in his youth, and which he enjoyed relating in after years as a partner in J. P. Morgan and Company. He had begun his business career as a low-paid bank teller with little prospect of promotion. Up to his window in the bank one day walked a tall gaunt stranger who thrust in a check. Davison studied it incredulously. The check read: "Pay to the order of Bearer, the Sum of Five Thousand Dollars," and it was signed, "Almighty God."

The young teller looked up to find himself confronted by the barrel of a revolver and a pair of blazing, maniacal eyes. He realized at once that if he made an error of judgment his life and perhaps the lives of others might be forfeited. To signal the bank guard was too risky, for banks in those days lacked the electrical warning signals that are now commonplace in tellers' cages. He hesitated only an instant. Then he said conversationally, "How would you like it—in hundreds?"

The man mumbled, "Yes." Davison reached for a stack of currency, meanwhile keeping his eyes steadily on the madman's, and said, "This is indeed an unusual privilege"—here he raised his voice a little—"to cash a check signed by Almighty God, and for five thousand dollars."

As he had hoped, his voice carried to the next cage. The teller there looked up, took in the situation, unobtrusively left his window, and walked around to the bank guard. Davison began to count out the money deliberately, looking up from time to time to hold the maniac's attention.

The guards came up quietly, and in a moment disarmed the man with the gun and led him out of the bank. Most of the other people present did not realize how near they had been to tragedy. The bank officers for the first time became aware of young Davison, and soon promoted him over the heads of his seniors to a job where his abilities could make themselves felt. He used to say that it would have taken him years longer to fight his way up the ladder if that lunatic had not come along.

HOW ENERGY PRODUCES PRESENCE OF MIND

Plainly enough, if Davison had responded to this unfavorable chance either by silently handing over the money or by yelling for help, the outcome would have been very different. Presence of mind enabled him to convert the chance into good luck. But now consider Davison's presence of mind from a physiological point of view. Modern science enables us to outline with reasonable certainty his physical and mental processes at the moment.

On the appearance of the armed madman, his adrenal glands responded by pumping adrenin into his bloodstream. This substance, with its remarkable property of calling forth glucose from the stores of the liver, mobilized his reserves of energy-yielding material. At the same time his powers of attention, instead of being turned inward upon his own fears, were sharply focused on the things he could see and hear; the unaware bank guard in the distance, the murmur of the voice of the teller in the next cage. His brain made a swift association of the facts. The result was a conscious perception that he might at the same time appease the madman and attract the attention of the teller. The high-energy content of his bloodstream and the power of his sympathetic nerve impulses enabled him to command his vocal chords successfully: he uttered the required words at the proper pitch, without undue excitement, and the result was luck.

The success of this intricate process depended, it is evident, on a high degree of energy. If Davison's brain, nervous system, or glandular system had been fatigued or sluggish, it is improbable that he could have made this speedy series of observations and associations and exercised his remarkable self-command. He showed courage, of course, but his presence of mind did not depend on courage. There are many courageous men who merely strike out blindly when chance confronts them with danger. Davison successfully responded to the chance because high energy of brain, nerves, and glands permitted him instantly to grasp the realities of the situation and adapt himself to them. This is the essential meaning of presence of mind.

The same process shows itself in cases of luck which do not involve any question of physical courage. Once Francis L. Wellman, the noted New York attorney, was presenting an involved lawsuit before a brusque judge who, failing to grasp its intricacies, decided that Wellman did not have a case, and refused to let it go to the jury. Wellman was not even permitted to call his witnesses, and when he rose to his feet to protest, the judge cut him short.

Crestfallen, Wellman sat down—or rather, tried to sit down. While he was talking someone had moved his chair, and he sprawled on the floor with a thud. Everybody roared, including the judge. Wellman rose, joined in the laughter, and then, taking advantage of the interruption, said, "Your Honor, I have just seen this case from a new angle. Will you allow me to present it?" Amused, and impressed by Wellman's poise, the judge let him speak, thought over what he said, and permitted one witness to testify. On hearing the testimony, he changed his mind about letting the case go before the jury—and Wellman won.

"Whenever any chance befalls you," wrote the Greek philosopher Epictetus, "remember to ask yourself how you can turn it to use." Presence of mind, founded in high energy, helps us to conceive our lucky responses to chance. No one, however excellent his character, can count on luck if he is chronically deficient in this quality. We tend to smile at the comic character of the absent-minded professor who is constantly getting into trouble, but absent-mindedness is not really funny, for it carries a potential of bad luck. Sometimes it may be due to intense intellectual concentration, but more often it bespeaks low energy reserves.

A typical incident was reported from a Pittsburgh war plant in 1943 by investigating officials of the War Production Board. Reports of low morale among the skilled workers of this plant, owing to a very high accident rate, proved authentic. It was found that a high proportion of accidents took place near the end of the shifts, especially overtime shifts. One worker, an operator of a machine cutting tool who had suffered a bad cut, told an investigator, "If I had been on my toes it would not have happened. A bolt loosened. It has happened plenty of times before, but this time I forgot to switch off the motor before reaching over to tighten it. I was thinking of my troubles, I guess." This man's record showed that he was a good worker, but owing to fatigue his mind had slid away from his work into an introspective pattern of thought. His absent-mindedness, or failure in presence of mind, needed only to be coupled with a small adverse chance to produce bad luck.

In this incident, we see two simple and positive clues to the way in which our luck can be protected against absence of mind. While we cannot always avoid fatigue, we can often avoid exposure to risks at times when our energies are low. If circumstances demand that we face those risks, fatigue or no, then *we need to try to throw our minds outward, away from ourselves, and to the external realities with which we must deal.* Mere awareness of the importance of presence of mind in chance situations can help us to generate the flow of the reserve energy that we need for lucky responses.

CONFIDENCE AND LUCK

When we turn to the second of the lucky attributes founded in our energy—confidence—we find yet greater scope for luck-development. There are specific means by which we can increase confidence. Two such means especially show their luck-value in case after case. They may be summed up in the words "preparation" and "suggestion."

The way in which preparation induces confidence and luck is suggested by a story once told by the late Walter P. Chrysler, founder of the huge motor company that bears his name. Chance brought to Chrysler's attention an apparently serious mistake made by an employee. Usually he left such matters in the hands of subordinates, but on this occasion he decided to send for the man and fire him personally. To his surprise, in the resulting interview he found his intended victim calm, collected, and confident. Vigorously the man defended his actions, standing up under hard questioning without yielding an inch or showing any sign of fear. He seemed to have complete faith that, when Chrysler heard the facts, he would approve what had been done. Chrysler was impressed. "I changed my mind about letting him go," he said. "I still wasn't sure he was right, and I knew he wasn't like that all the time, but I figured if he could be like that when it mattered, I wanted him."

Undoubtedly this employee had thought long and hard about his defense and was fully prepared to answer Chrysler's attack. If he had faltered at any point, the decision would almost certainly have been against him. The preparatory energy which he had put into his defense resulted in his attitude of confidence; and his confidence made Chrysler question his own preconceived judgment, and so change his mind.

Especially in those instances which involve other people, *preparatory study of the facts makes for luck*. If the brain conveys an emphatic message—"You know more than the others"—this is enough to set up in the sympathetic nervous and glandular systems a train of responses which finally tap the energy reserves. When these are sufficient the entire body chemistry is affected, and the result is the vigorous blood flow, the erect bearing, the unconstricted breathing, the shining eyes, the relaxed facial muscles and natural smile that bespeak the confident man.

That no one is confident all the time, or in the face of all chances, we can take for granted. The normal ebb and flow of energy reduces confidence at certain periods, especially at night when the body is fatigued and when worry and fear tend to rise in us. To try to whip up energy when we are tired, to flog ourselves to further work when our body cries for rest, and where there is no particular challenge to be met, would be to weaken, not to build, confidence. Our need is to *use periods of high energy to prepare for the chances of life that seem most probable*. The potential of luck thus created may be tapped by chance at a much later time. The important point is that whenever the right chance comes along, it should find us confident and capable of energetic response.

We see this principle at work in the case of Alva Johnston, the brilliant journalist. In 1921, when he was a young *New York Times* reporter, Johnston read a questionnaire written by Thomas Edison to enable laymen to determine whether they knew as much as they should about science. Dissatisfied with his score in this test, and feeling that every good journalist ought to have a working knowledge of science, he doggedly undertook the systematic reading of scientific books and periodicals. A year later this energetic effort of preparation combined with chance to produce luck. Carr Van Anda, then managing editor of the great newspaper, heard that the American Association for the Advancement of Science was to hold an important meeting in Cambridge, Massachusetts. He looked around the city room, and his eyes fell on Johnston. A short time earlier this assignment might have appalled Johnston, but now he accepted it with confidence. The result was a remarkable series of articles on a wide variety of scientific subjects, which won him the Pulitzer Prize and brought him to national prominence in his field.

BUILDING CONFIDENCE
THROUGH SUGGESTION

The psychological root of confidence, we know, lies in a sense of security. Obviously, secure people are not sure of themselves at all times. Obviously again, insecure people may feel confident and lucky in certain situations. Yet when we see a man with a prevailing attitude of confidence, we usually discover a mind relatively free from harrowing anxiety. As experience soon teaches, anxiety insidiously consumes our energy, and dangerously weakens our responses to chance.

The plain fact is that most of us are not very secure, and most of us suffer from anxiety a good part of the time. How, then, are we to keep confidence high? To gain psychological security when one has not got it requires a long leap upward. Though it may occasionally be achieved through life experience, or through psychoanalysis, we cannot count on such a major transformation in our lives. Nevertheless, even those who suffer from chronic anxiety have a means of strengthening their confidence in the face of risky chances—*the power of suggestion*.

We are suggestible beings, most of us—easily encouraged or discouraged before the big tests of life. With a wise and lucky instinct, we seek to expose ourselves to influences which reinforce our confidence. We turn to the optimist who tells us, "You can do it," rather than to the "realist" who calculates our probability of failure. Nothing could be more sensible. The friend who sends us to our task with a cheery word helps to release our reserve of energy, while the skeptic fills our mind with doubt, which blocks the energy flow that might carry us to luck. It is worth noting that even so famous and successful an actress as Katharine Cornell refuses to read adverse critical notices of her plays after opening nights lest they diminish her enthusiasm and energy.

We see the extraordinary power of suggestion to overcome anxiety and induce confidence in an experience of the distinguished illustrator, Edward A. Wilson. Public speaking to Wilson has always been a terrifying ordeal, but on one occasion he was so strongly pressed to make a speech at an important dinner of writers and artists that he found no way of refusing. The day of the speech found him deeply depressed at the prospect, to the point where he thought he would not be able to go through with it. He had not even thought of anything that seemed to him worth saying, and only his sense of responsibility prevented him from becoming suddenly ill.

That day friends persuaded him to lunch with them. Making a conscious effort to be cheerful, so as not to inflict his troubles on others, he began to reminisce about old Bohemian days in Chicago, where he had worked as a young artist. The enthusiastic laughter of his friends made him wonder, for the first time, whether he might not, after all, be able to entertain a larger audience. Later, he scrawled a brief account of his Chicago beginnings in art and gave it to a public stenographer to type for him. When she handed it back, she commented, "That's a swell speech. I type a lot of them, and I know."

This remark was a psychological turning point. With the suggestion of success working in him, Wilson was able to rise to his feet at the dinner without the sense of panic that he had anticipated, and he utterly astounded himself by charming and delighting his audience. He refers to the incident as lucky, as indeed it was: the luck arose in large measure from the interplay of chance and the power of suggestion.

In sports, of course, suggestion is a familiar instrument for inducing confidence and luck. The football coach tells his flagging team, "You cant lose!" and sometimes galvanizes them into a new burst of energy. Some team coaches try to arouse anger by scorn, and so release the energy reserves of their men, since anger has an effect on glandular chemistry similar to hope. "Beware of a rabbit in a rage!" wrote William Blake, and today psychologists, with their theory of overcompensation, echo his thought.

When a timid man forgets his fears and acts as though he cannot fail, he will often amaze. The David and Goliath stories of history have all begun when an underdog forgot he was an underdog and drew on unsuspected reserves of power to produce luck.

Confidence-building suggestion does not always have to come through others. Many people successfully practice autosuggestion before facing serious tests. Not long ago a businessman was summoned to Washington for a hearing before a Congressional committee on certain suspected violations of law. He thought he was in the right, but his company's future was at stake and he was frankly worried. Shortly before the hearing, he disappeared. His assistants were alarmed. Finally he strode into the committee room—and their alarm subsided. They had seen that look on his face before. There was a grim smile on his face and a fighting glint in his eye. He radiated power. He met every question shot at him with good-humored vigor. He came through the inquisition in triumph. Even the Congressmen who had been against him applauded at the end.

Afterward this man told his friends that in the half-hour before the session he had "worked on himself." "I took a walk," he said, "and kept telling myself, 'These Congressmen are reasonable people. You've got the facts. You know the answers. This is what they'll say. This is what you'll say. You can't lose! Why, it's in the bag! You'll show those birds!'"

Within limits, this is sound luck-practice. It will be recalled that the French physician Coué once created a vogue by persuading thousands of people, mostly women, to stand each morning in front of mirrors and repeat for five minutes, "Every day in every way I am getting better and better." However bizarre the technique employed, his basic idea was not without foundation. There are probably millions of people who employ similar methods on occasion, telling themselves, or getting others to tell them, "You can do it!" "You are abler than you think!" Some people have even gone so far as to employ hypnotists to feed the assurance they wanted to the unconscious mind in the trance state.

Another common form of autosuggestion which plays a part in a number of luck-stories is the improvement of one's physical appearance. The relation between appearance and confidence has a firm physiological basis. It is now well established that the muscles, by their degree of tension, can affect the sympathetic nervous system, and so create emotion as well as respond to it. Thus, by physically simulating an emotion, it is sometimes possible to induce it; if a man holds himself erect, firms his jaw, looks people in the eye, and smiles, he may be able to generate a feeling of confidence.

The shy girl who, on the eve of her first date, practices her most appealing expressions and most graceful walk in front of a mirror eases her anxiety by demonstrating her attractiveness to herself. Another technique of the same sort involves dressing the part of the successful, and hence presumably confident person. Many a tired woman facing a social evening has achieved an extraordinary release of reserve energy by beautifying herself; and applicants for jobs frequently make themselves more confident by sartorially suggesting to others and to themselves that they have no worries.

It should be added, however, that the experience of some who have used autosuggestion techniques indicates that while the results are not insignificant, they are usually short-lived. The glands and nerves apparently respond a few times to such devices, but seem to catch on quickly and presently learn to ignore the simulations of confidence. Full confidence arises only when the brain's realistic anticipation of probable success taps the energy reserves. This generally means that we have prepared for the test—and it is then that luck hovers near us.

DETERMINATION AND
THE RENEWAL OF ENERGY

Like confidence and presence of mind, a third lucky quality, determination (in the sense of fixed purpose), is also normally associated with high energy. Why are some men more determined than others in carrying through a given activity? The answer almost always lies in the fact that they are able to renew their energy in relation to that activity. Many a man who is capable of high energy when he first tackles a given enterprise finds that if it requires repeated effort he can no longer muster the requisite vigor for the task, and so he drops it. A single adverse chance can therefore defeat him. But a man who is able to sustain high energy in successive attempts can often achieve a lucky conclusion the second or third time. While confidence demands the use of energy in preparation, and presence of mind requires a specific concentration of energy in the face of chance, *determination grows out of the repeated tapping of the energy reserves in the pursuit of a single purpose.*

We see the workings of this process, together with its lucky consequences, in a story related by the local doctor in a small town in New York State—a vital, cheery man, with a strong foreign accent. He had come there from Germany not long before, and when asked to explain why he had chosen that out-of-the-way spot for his practice, he said:

"My wife and I came to America in 1933. It was a bad time in Germany, but we found it was also a bad time here. Especially for German doctors. There were many like me, and not enough places to work. Because I had had a good education and record in Germany, I was granted a license to practice, but how could I hope to find patients in New York, where I knew nobody? As for the hospitals, they were then not able even to absorb all the talented young doctors from American schools, and of course they could not be expected to offer me a post. My wife and I were very worried. We had a little money, but not enough to last long. But it was no use to sit around and wring our hands. Instead, since I was not working, we decided to see something of the countryside. We bought a little used car and began to make short tours. What we saw, we liked. It was better than the city, and my wife said, 'Why not be a country doctor?'

"I told her, 'Be sensible. How can I, with my accent, hope to be a doctor in a place where foreigners are regarded with suspicion? Besides, you can be sure that every country town already has doctors. I would not even know where to begin to look.'

"Once my wife gets an idea in her head, you cannot do

much about it. From that moment, every time we stopped for gas, or for a meal, she would ask the attendant or the waitress, 'Do they need a doctor in this town?' Of course, they thought she was crazy, and they said no, there already was a Dr. Smith or Jones or Brown. I begged her to stop. I said, 'Please, Hilda, it is embarrassing.' But she paid no attention. She is the kind of woman who must always be doing something. Otherwise she is unhappy. It got so I hated to drive into a filling station, because as soon as the man came up, out would come that question, 'Do you need a doctor here?'

"After several weeks of this, even Hilda began to be discouraged. One day we were driving, and I said, 'Hilda, it is no use. Give up that nonsense.' And she said, 'Perhaps you are right.' Right after that we stopped for gas, near here. I saw Hilda take a deep breath, and before I could stop her, she asked her question. To my amazement, the man scratched his head and said, 'Funny you should ask that. The old doc just got sick and died the other day, and we're kind of thinking we better get somebody else real quick.'

"Hilda said to me, 'You see?' And so we came here, and I talked with people, and set up an office. Everything has been fine since then. We have many friends and we never want to live anywhere else."

Again and again in life, determination applied to a specific purpose, after numerous failures, touches the one chance needed to produce luck. When this happens, we usually find two circumstances: (1) the person concerned kept his (or her) purpose constantly in sight, repeatedly stimulating hope and renewing incentive and generating energy; (2) he prevented himself from growing stale through an occasional change of activity, which made possible a zestful return to the attack. It is a significant point of the story just related that the doctor and his wife had a sufficient variety and change of interest between trips so that she never became bored with her quest.

INCREASING OUR TOTAL ENERGY

Through determination, through confidence and presence of mind, energy plays a vital role in our luck. Again and again in life we see that when lucky responses to chance flow naturally and spontaneously from a person, it is because at least one of these three attributes is strongly marked in his personality. These energy-founded qualities can be strengthened in any of us by conscious use of the techniques discussed above.

When all this is said, the fact still remains that the problem of keeping energy high for luck is not entirely, or even primarily, a matter of such techniques. High energy, with its potential of good fortune, is to some extent a manifestation of ready-made luck. People are like automobiles in that, from the moment of production, some have a higher horsepower rating than others. By physical inheritance and early conditioning one man will develop as a high-energy person, whereas another, through no fault of his own, will be relatively deficient in the power of work.

Yet energy is not, after all, a tangible characteristic, like hair on the chest. *High energy is in large degree the expression of an attitude toward life.* An improvement in state of mind, such as results from the shaking off of anxiety, can go far to increase available energy. And there are other ways. "A single successful effort of moral volition," wrote William James, "such as saying 'no' to some habitual temptation, or performing some courageous act, will launch a man on a higher level of energy for days or weeks, will give him a new range of power."

A major step in luck-development lies in learning how to get the best out of ones potential of energy, whatever its horsepower rating, and how to use it to best advantage in responding to life's chances. While it is undeniable that the Cadillac is a better automobile than the Chevrolet, it is also true that the skill of the drivers can make a profound difference in the lives of the cars. A well-driven

Chevrolet may last longer and run better than a badly driven Cadillac; and a person of lesser energy can by its conservation and skillful application sometimes accomplish more, and be luckier, than someone of higher native energy who expends it on meaningless pursuits. We human beings, gifted as we are with consciousness, can decide to some extent how we shall drive the physical machines which we inherited from our parents.

The wonderful and encouraging fact is that slight improvements in elementary techniques of living can often raise our available energy and luck-potential in a very short time. This is not the place for a full discussion of the effects on health and energy of diet, exercise, sleep, and state of mind. It must be emphatically said, however, that *anyone who fails to make an effort to eat and drink wisely, to get enough exercise and rest, and to shake off his worries greatly weakens his power to respond successfully to life's chances.* Any effort that we make to raise the level of our energy by improvement in these essential aspects of living automatically tends to raise our luck-potential.

We shall deal further with the specific effort that can transform our luck in the Conclusion of this book. At this point, it is well to bear in mind that, important as energy is in our responses to chance, we do not have to be paragons of power to be lucky. In fact, from time to time astonishing luck is experienced by people whose energy is acutely subnormal. When that happens, the reason lies in the strength of other characteristics, which also tend to produce effective responses to chance. Luck is a many-sided marvel, and can be approached by numerous routes. Not less direct than energy is the route of imagination, to which we now turn.

3

IMAGINATION AND LUCK

". . . As imagination bodies forth the
forms of things unknown . . ."

SHAKESPEARE

A customer drove into a gas station in western Pennsylvania and was surprised to have his car serviced by a one-armed attendant. Chatting with the owner of the station, he admired the dexterity of the crippled man, and remarked that he seemed to get along better than many men with two arms. "From my standpoint, a lot better," said the owner, and told the story. Some months before, the one-armed youngster, fresh from an Army hospital, had driven up to the station in an old jalopy to buy gasoline. While the tank was being filled, he had dejectedly remarked to the owner that he had been trying to get a job, but nobody seemed to want a one-armed man. Did the owner by any chance need help?

"Need it, but can't afford to pay for it," the owner said. At that moment a big car drove into the station, and the woman driver peremptorily demanded gas. The owner, a man of independent spirit, replied, " 'Tend to you as soon as I'm through with this car, lady." Annoyed, the woman was about to drive away when the one-armed youth said, "I'll fill her tank if you like"—and proceeded to do so, neatly and efficiently. Watching, the owner saw the woman's angry frown vanish and her face soften. Now his imagination was stimulated or, as he put it, "I suddenly woke up." That is to say, he began to visualize the ex-soldier in an attendant's uniform, the sympathetic attitude of customers, the word-of-mouth advertising that the station would get in the locality. "I figured it would work out, and it has," he went on. "There are some things he can't do very well, like changing tires, but anything else he handles O.K. The word got around, and a lot of new people have been coming in on account of they like the idea of my hiring him."

At the core of this incident is an imaginative perception, which enabled the owner to grasp the possibilities of a chance, and so respond to it effectively. Not a very big feat of imagination, certainly, but it sufficed to make possible a lucky decision.

Wherever luck is most impressive, it is usually because

energy has been directed by imagination, which reveals the potentialities of a chance. Combining memory of things past with observation of things before us, imagination enables us to envisage things and situations not present to the senses. In this way, it not only guides us to luck but fills life with the color and excitement that save it from drab monotony. The poet sees a skylark and imagines an ode; the housewife sees an empty room and furnishes it in her mind; the businessman sees a plot of barren land and pictures it with houses and streets; the inventor watches a kite and dreams of an airplane. The highest values of human experience and achievement depend in one degree or another on imagination.

EGOCENTRIC AND HEALTHY IMAGINATION

Not every imagination, as we all know, makes for good luck. Notably, the egocentric imagination, which evokes images concerned primarily with selfish gratifications, breeds unluckiness. One of its distinguishing products is the daydream—the fantasy which is always concerned with the future of the dreamer and which leads to the fictional fulfillment of some desire. In children it is usually the desire for power and recognition that provides the "castle in the air"; in adults the daydreams broaden their subject matter to embrace sex, security, self-expression, and other desires. It is of course normal for everyone to daydream from time to time. Occasionally, when these egocentric imaginings are accompanied by creative talent, they may give rise to artistic efforts.

But heedlessly indulged, the daydream can be a menace to good luck. It weakens one's hold on reality and reduces the energy available for the real tasks of life, making them seem distasteful by comparison with the rosy images of the mind. We smile at the girl with the Cinderella daydream who refuses to help her mother with the dishes because she dreams of herself as a princess-to-be, and at the young man who pictures himself sailing the seas on a steam yacht with a harem of Hollywood beauties, but fantasies like these are funny only when they are infrequent and soon put aside. Long continued, they tend to put blinders on the mind, making it difficult to perceive the nature of chances that cross the line of vision. Some people even come to see their favorite fantasies with such clarity of focus as to believe them real, and hallucination follows.

In addition to the habitual daydream, there is another unlucky way in which the egocentric imagination often expresses itself—morbidity. We all know people who habitually "imagine the worst." Usually the reason lies in deep-rooted feelings of anxiety. The morbid imagination tends to combine only the unpleasant perceptions that fit into its dark and distorted picture of life, and to ignore any cheerful elements. Where this condition exists, a trivial chance can easily produce a major increase of unhappiness. In illustration, we have the case of a woman who could not see her husband go on a business trip without being overtaken by jealous and groundless imaginings, in which she saw him in the arms of other women. She was combining three ideas: her husband was out of her sight; many men are not faithful to their wives; there were women in the city to which he had gone. However, she left out of her imaginative synthesis other facts, equally important: her husband was straightforward and devoted; he was extremely busy and had no time for philandering.

His earnest attempts to reassure her were unavailing; and in this dark state of mind, she had opened the way for bad luck through any unfavorable chance. The chance came when her path crossed that of an acquaintance of her husband's, one of those all-too-common jokers who think it amusing to hint at presumptive infidelities of wife and husband. This jealous wife was an easy target.

Only a few sly remarks were needed to produce an effect on her. She went home in a torment of doubt. Unable to bear her jealousy, she caught a plane to the city where her husband was and walked unannounced into his hotel room, breaking into an important business conference. The interruption and his chagrin and embarrassment unnerved him and prevented him from completing the deal on which he was working. The result was anger, a violent quarrel, and a sharp deterioration in their relationship, which ended in divorce a year later.

The unmistakable characteristic of the healthy and lucky imagination is that it readily turns outward, away from the self. It does not confuse the world of external reality with the images conjured up by desire or anxiety. Consequently, its images, even when highly colored, have roots in things as they are or will be. As might be expected, men of great accomplishment almost always display strong and active imagination. They are able to make unusual combinations of things remembered and observed within the framework of reality; and so their images and ideas frequently strike a note of originality. Such was the imagination of Henry Ford, who combined knowledge of production methods with knowledge of the economics of the market to conceive of the first mass-produced, low-priced automobile. Such was the imagination of Dr. Walter Reed, when he visualized a mosquito as the carrier of the dreaded yellow fever; and, at an extraordinary level, of Albert Einstein, when he grasped the symbolic logic of the relationship between energy and mass which underlies the development of atomic power.

THE LUCK-VALUE OF EMPATHIC IMAGINATION

Of all expressions of imagination, none so frequently reveals itself in case histories of luck as that human attribute which is called empathy by the psychologists. It is empathy that enables us to share the feelings of others in given situations, and provides the foundation of such emotions as compassion and sympathetic joy. It is empathy that makes our muscles tense when we look at the tightrope walker doing a perilous stunt; that brings a smile to our faces when we see someone else laughing, even when we do not know why; that causes us to wince when the batter is struck by a pitched ball; and to feel embarrassment when the unsuspecting contestant in a television show is "put on the spot" by a ruthless master of ceremonies. Empathy is again at work in our responses to things we read and hear; it is when we can identify ourselves with the characters of a play or a story that we are most moved. "The feeling for others" is part of our social instinct, of our inheritance as gregarious beings.

How the strong empathic imagination leads to good luck is suggested by the experience of a private secretary in New York City, Miss M. W. The incident took place soon after she was graduated from business school and while she was looking for her first job. She was one of several girls who answered an advertisement for a secretary in a small manufacturing company. As she entered the reception room she heard an angry voice say, "You can tell him for me I'm sick of waiting and he can go to hell"—and a scowling man stormed past her. Several other girls, also applicants for the secretarial job, were already sitting in the room, and were startled by the man's outburst. Miss W. remembers that she heard one of them whisper to another, "I wish I could afford to do that." As Miss W. sat down, the harassed office receptionist delivered a censored version of the man's message to her boss, Mr. L., over the interoffice telephone.

This Mr. L. was Miss W.'s prospective employer. She had half an hour to wait before her interview and in that time she did some hard thinking. When Mr. L. sent for her and began to ask the usual questions, she said, "You will find many girls who can do shorthand as well as I, and who have had more experience. But in these days stenography is pretty much a routine accomplishment. Don't you feel that being able to deal with people is equally important for a secretary? I've given a good deal of thought to the art of keeping people cheerful and friendly, especially when things go wrong or when they feel badly treated for any reason."

The incident of the angry, forgotten man was still in Mr. L.'s mind. With his attention diverted from Miss W.'s inexperience to her personality, he began to talk to her of his problems, and ended by giving her the job.

Chance offered Miss W. an advantageous glimpse of Mr. L's secretarial needs. But the other girls who had been interviewed before her had had the same glimpse, and it brought them no luck. It was the imaginative response of Miss W.'s mind that carried the chance to the point where it affected her interests, and so became luck.

One of the significant points in this little story is the whispered remark made by one of the other applicants, and overheard by Miss W. From this remark, we can almost reconstruct the state of mind of the girl who made it. Consider her position. Like the angry man, she had been kept waiting. She was, moreover, in the somewhat uncomfortable position of applying for a job—that is, submitting herself and her future to the judgment of a stranger—a situation which does some violence to the ego. It was both easy and natural for her to identify herself with the angry man and his protest.

For years, one may surmise, she had secretly hankered to speak her mind to office receptionists and high-handed executives who ordered her around. For an instant, empathy gave her the pleasant feeling of having done so vicariously. But, as her remark to Miss W. showed, her mind swiftly reverted to the fact that she could not afford to express herself that way. She wished that she could, but no doubt she needed the job. At this moment, in all probability, recollections of her domestic and economic problems floated through her consciousness, and old anxieties possessed her. With her mind thus turned inward, and her spirits lowered, she could not respond effectively to the chance of the angry man, even though she may have dimly recognized its bearing on her present situation.

Miss W. recalled that she too felt at first a feeling of identification with the angry man. Next, she felt a twinge of sympathy for the receptionist who had the unpleasant task of telling Mr. L. what had happened. Then the thought came: "How will this affect Mr. L.?" Would the receptionist's report have a disagreeable effect on his mind, and so possibly prejudice Miss W.'s chances of getting the job? Mr. L. was evidently a busy and harassed man. Could she perhaps say something to him which would convey her understanding of his problem, and so put him in a better frame of mind? In seeking to answer this question, her mind produced the ideas and phrases that caught Mr. L.'s attention and won her her job.

IDENTIFICATION,
UNDERSTANDING, AND LUCK

The crux of this process lay in Miss W.'s ability to identify herself not only with the man whom she had seen but also with a man she had not seen. Once the angry man had left, her mind then was bound to move on, either to consideration of self or to some other aspect of the external situation. Miss W.'s mind took the latter, and lucky, route. She projected herself imaginatively into Mr. L.'s position and saw the problem from his point of view. Unlike the other girl, she did not think in egocentric terms. Although she too had serious personal problems, she did not indulge in self-pity, and felt no resurgence of anxiety. Nor, having thought of Mr. L., did she fall into the common trap of daydreaming, weaving a fantasy in which he turned out to be a handsome bachelor and fell in love with her. Her imagination held to the line of objective reality. Mr. L. plainly needed a certain kind of help in his work. By stressing her abilities in that direction, she might make him more lenient to her inexperience.

The importance of the empathic imagination in luck-development grows out of a fact already noted—that a great part of human luck depends on other people. When we share their states of mind, we are more likely to respond to chances in ways which link them to us emotionally, making for a greater probability of luck for all concerned. Many lucky incidents have begun when one person felt sympathy with another's misfortune. To take a commonplace example: The owner of a women's dress shop saw an employee who was carrying an expensive dress accidentally catch the hem on a sharp table corner and tear it. His first impulse, he recalls, was to reprimand her, but looking at her alarmed face, and at the faces of his other salespeople, he sensed their common distress and changed his mind. Instead, he passed the incident off lightly.

"Happens to all of us," he said. "Don't worry about it. We'll try to mend the dress." The result of this casual response to a trivial chance astonished him. At this one display of imaginative understanding, the previously indifferent attitude of his employees toward him seemed to change. They began to display more interest in their work than ever before. On his birthday, which came soon afterward, he was taken aback when his staff held an impromptu little celebration and gave him a gift. He began to find more pleasure in his own work. "As far as I am concerned," he related, "it was lucky when that dress got torn." The essential point is that empathic imagination saved him from making a response to the chance that would have caused pain, and directed him to a response that produced good feeling.

Again and again in life a lucky outcome results from a perfectly ordinary chance situation simply because it has been touched with the magical wand of empathic imagination. Perhaps in no area of life is this truer than in relations between the sexes. In a typical case, a young man remarks that his successful marriage grew out of a chance meeting at a theater box office. Standing in line to buy tickets, he saw a beautiful girl behind the window grating. He was normally rather shy, but as he put it, "I happened to be feeling wonderful. It was a bright, sunny day, my job was going well, and life seemed full of promise. When my turn at the window came and I asked for tickets, the girl never even looked at me. All of a sudden I got the notion that with the bars in the windows and all the gaping people outside, she must feel like a caged animal in the zoo. So I said that. She laughed, and said that the bars helped to keep the wolves away. That was all for the moment, but later, when the crowd was gone. I went back and asked her if she would go to the zoo with me and see how the other animals lived. By that time, we felt as if we knew each other, and she said yes, and that's when our good luck got under way."

The young man's first remark at the window showed a degree of understanding, as well as exuberance, a fact which took it out of the category of the ordinary male bid for attention. Empathic imagination always tends to create favorable awareness in others, but its attractive power is probably strongest when a man and a woman are brought together by chance. Women especially, knowing how much their happiness depends on the understanding of their mates, seem instinctively to respond to evidences of strong empathy in the men they meet.

Again, in the relations between parents and children, a high degree of imaginative identification can often produce lifelong luck. The parent who can project himself into the mind of a child—who realizes that the great events of a child's life often appear inconsequential to adults—will sometimes by a single action or remark contribute enormously to the child's sense of security and later luckiness.

Significant in this connection is the recollection of one man, exceptionally happy and well adjusted, who grew up in straitened circumstances on a small farm. In his own words: "I think my luckiest experience happened when I was about seven years old. It was a spring day, and I recall going to the orchard and seeing the apple blossoms in sudden bloom. It was a beautiful sight and I was tremendously excited. I shall never forget my father's saying to me, 'That's why we never have to be afraid of anything. Nature is there with a fresh crop every year.' That may not sound very profound, but I can't tell you how much those words meant to me then, and how much strength and comfort I have derived from them since." In this little incident lies a clue to the direction from which good luck is most likely to strike into the lives of children. *If the child's parents are imaginatively aware of his need for psychological security, they take a long step toward better luck for him and for the entire family.*

HOW PREJUDICE BREEDS BAD LUCK

As a strong empathic imagination can bring good luck out of unfavorable or run-of-mine chances, so a weakness in this department of the personality can lead to disastrous failures—even in situations which, in the beginning, seem full of bright promise. The history of politics, for example, is crowded with the stories of statesmen who tumbled from eminence to limbo because they could not identify themselves with ordinary people and sense their needs, hopes, and thoughts. Especially, the evidence makes it clear that irrational prejudice—social snobbishness, religious bigotry, and class or race consciousness—always carries the seeds of misfortune. Major obstacles to the free flow of empathic feeling, these states of mind generate unnecessary hostilities, so that the snob, the bigot, and the fanatic always stand high on the list of candidates for misfortune.

Even among businessmen, who are usually not espe-

cially interested in each other's private beliefs, the relationship between prejudice and bad luck is unmistakable.
A revealing case is that of an unreconstructed rebel from
Texas who, in discussing the subject of luck, said flatly,
"The best luck anybody can have is to be born a white,
Protestant American. Otherwise he is out of luck." Now
it is an undoubted fact that in a world full of prejudice
ready-make luck does to an extent hinge on color, race,
nationality, and religion. On the other hand, a little common sense tells us that there is no guarantee of good luck
in any such formula as this man put forth. The mere fact
that he held such distinctions in the forefront of his mind
was a danger sign. As was to be expected, he made no
secret of his hostility toward Negroes, Jews, and Catholics.

In time, the company for which he worked invited him
to a convention in Atlantic City. There he learned that, in
arranging hotel accommodations, the president of the
company had decided to promote good fellowship by having every room shared by two men, each from a different
section of the country. A quiet-spoken young man from
Boston, with a pleasant manner and an Irish name, was
the Texan's roommate. It was not hard to guess that he was
a Catholic. Trying to be agreeable, and seeking a common
ground of interest, the Southerner soon confided his feelings about Negroes and Jews. The Bostonian merely said,
"I don't feel that way," and let the matter drop. It was plain

to him that the word "Catholic" had been omitted only out of courtesy.

A few months later the Bostonian was promoted to an important executive post in the company. The Texan had been agitating for an extension of his sales territory to include the southern part of Louisiana, an arrangement which would have meant a large addition to his income, and to which his previous sales record seemed to entitle him. The matter came to the attention of a committee of which the Bostonian was a member. He voted against it, giving it as his view that the strong prejudices of the Texan would work against him in a state where the Catholic, Negro, and Jewish populations were substantial. The rest of the committee agreed.

The Texan was not informed of the real reason for the refusal of his request, but it embittered him, and his sub-sequent career was full of trouble. Chance had brought the two men together—the artificial distinctions in the Southerner's mind had prevented his imagination from revealing to him how the other felt; and the result was bad luck.

His experience, while perhaps unusual in detail, was not in the least exceptional in its general character. The creeping vine of intolerance always grows in the dark places of the mind, where the light of empathic imagina-tion cannot reach it, and it always bears bitter fruit. Chance can direct the potential of misfortune in prejudice against the hater as easily as against the hated.

For prejudice dwells in insecure minds, which, as we have seen, are natural targets for trouble.

DEVELOPING THE LUCKY IMAGINATION

With deep and beautiful insight, Dante wrote,

> By so many more there are who say "ours,"
> So much the more of good doth each possess.

The words repay our utmost thought. Everyone has his psychological "we-group"—the people with whom he usually identifies himself. In group relations, as in individual lives, we make ourselves luckier as we free ourselves from egocentric attitudes.

Situations in which men isolate themselves in spirit from other men, and indulge feelings of superiority and hostility, are notoriously prone to end unluckily. A contemptuous expression on the face of an industrialist when he talked to a labor leader has been known to produce a costly strike. Many a disastrous war has broken out because men were so wrapped up in the feelings of their own group that they could not imagine how others felt and thought. It is only when we make a conscious effort to understand the point of view of those whom we conceive as enemies that we do our utmost to avoid the misfortune of war.

The barrier of artificial group distinctions blocks the path to better luck for nations and individuals alike. The wise man learns early to surmount this barrier. Instead of puffing himself up with stiff-necked pride in belonging to a certain family, nation, race, religion, or social group, he uses his imagination to broaden his we-group, and so invites better luck into his life.

There are simple and direct ways of developing the empathic faculty. One way is to read books which deal wisely and straightforwardly with this problem, such as Dr. Harry A. Overstreet's *The Mature Mind*. A more individualized method of increasing our powers of indentification with others is suggested by the experience of a young short-story writer. Early in his career he had an illuminating talk with a perceptive editor, who said to him, "I don't feel that your characters live in these stories. The reader can't identify himself with them. The reason, I suspect, is that you never really felt their feelings, while you were writing about them."

The young writer knew this criticism to be true. It came to him that if he was to do better, he must be able to project himself more fully into the minds of his characters. His education was spotty, and his experience of life meager, but he decided to try an experiment. He invented a sort of empathic discipline for himself. Each day he would select one person whom he knew, or had seen, and whose walk of life was different from his own, and he would try to put himself imaginatively into that person's situation as he had observed it. At first, he made little headway. His own attitudes and beliefs kept getting in the way of the identification. As time went on, however, now and then he was able to visualize in some detail the circumstances of a given life and to sense some of the resulting emotions in the mind of another. This game that he assiduously played, he found, was of more help in giving him understanding of his fellow men than he had believed possible, and the subsequent success of his work testified to the value of the effort.

Often the imagination does not need so conscious and strenuous an effort in order to expand; a single chance remark may help to unleash its power. In a not unusual case, a former machinery salesman, later a sales manager, remarked that he was a failure as a salesman until one day a customer told him, "I don't care how many years it took to perfect this machine. What I want to know is, what will it do for me?" It dawned on him then that he had been approaching his job entirely in terms of his own interests, which were primarily technical. For the first time he began to wonder what went on in a prospective customer's mind—to identify himself with the other fellow. With the identification came insight into the things that the prospect wanted to know, and awareness of the objections in his mind. "I learned how to answer his objections before he had a chance to spout them," this man recalled. "And instead of telling him how proud we were of our ultra-accurate machining, I talked to him about the things that interested him—savings, profits. That was when I began to go places."

Whatever the approach taken, everyone stands to benefit from effort to strengthen the empathic faculty. To begin requires only a slight extension of normal curiosity. We all wonder from time to time what goes on in the minds of others. To move from mere wondering to a conscious attempt at identification is not a great step. When we seriously try to enter into the thoughts and emotions of other people—especially people on the far side of our mental barriers—we make it easier for luck to help us fulfill our basic desires in life.

4

THE LUCKINESS OF FAITH

"Let us put on the armor of light."

ROMANS

The qualities of mind which intertwine with the chances of life to produce good luck at its most spectacular are dramatically revealed in the story of a Polish girl, of noble family, who fled from her country when it was invaded by the German armies in 1939 and came to England. Speaking both English and French fluently, she was quickly accepted for service with the British forces, and carefully trained. Two years later she was parachuted into southern France to serve as radio operator on the staff of a young British officer, who had been helping to organize the powerful French resistance movement against the German occupation.

This officer, Lt. Col. Francis Cammaerts, one of the heroes of World War II, was a legendary figure of the French underground. Frequently pursued by German raiding parties, he had always escaped in time; but one day in 1944 an evening patrol stopped Cammaerts and two English aides as they rode through a forest on bicycles, disguised as French peasants. Although their papers were in order, and all three spoke French like natives, some circumstance aroused suspicion. The men were arrested and thrown into jail in the town of Digne; and the local German garrison commander, suspecting that he had three *Maquisards* who had been picking off his troops and destroying his munitions, announced that they would be shot the next evening, August 16.

When the Polish girl heard of the death sentence, her mind wrestled with the seemingly impossible problem: how to save the three Englishmen? Brought up in a strong, mystical faith, and animated by motives of high idealism, she had a conviction that she might succeed. Allied progress in northern France, she knew, must be causing fear in the hearts of many German soldiers of the reckoning which might come to them when the country was liberated. Could she trade on that fear?

She determined to try. Among the Frenchmen of Digne whom she knew was a gendarme, secretly patriotic but regarded as a collaborationist by the Germans, who had been assigned as a guard at the local Occupation headquarters. Through him, the girl learned a number of facts about the German officer in command—where he came from, his street address, his wife's name, how many children he had, and much more. The next day she walked into the officer's room at headquarters and amazed him by introducing herself as an English spy, and still more with the assertion that she was the niece of Field Marshal Montgomery—this last being a pure fabrication.

Her purpose was to startle him into attention, and she succeeded. She then said that the three men sentenced to death were the most important British officers in France—as indicated by the fact that she had been assigned to work with them. She had now been instructed over the short-wave radio from London, she went on, to convey this message: if these men were shot, the German military establishment at Digne would be bombed into extinction. Moreover, the German officer would be held personally responsible. The British knew who he was, where he lived, and all about him, and reprisal would be exacted not only from him but from his family.

Here she cited the facts that she had learned about the officer, which visibly shook him. The fall of Germany was inevitable, she went on to say, now that the Allied Army was on the Continent in force. Within the next few hours, another army would invade the south of France, Digne would be captured, and the officer, if he carried out the execution, would be held as a war criminal, and all his family property confiscated. This again was wholly invented; the girl had no knowledge whatsoever of Allied invasion plans.

The German was half convinced, but only half. He did not believe the Allies would reach southern France for a long while to come. If he released these men, he would inevitably get into trouble with his own superiors—and no small trouble. Impressed by the girl's courage, he listened courteously to her; they talked for several hours, but at the end he ordered her arrest.

That luck could save her, or the imperiled Englishmen, seemed altogether unlikely; yet she had created a situation in which a favoring chance, should it arrive, could still effect a rescue. Here the needed, spectacular coincidence shot into the crisis—a radio message, handed to the startled officer at that very moment, stating that an American army had just landed on the southern coast of France. Hardly a minute later a squadron of American planes roared overhead, reinforcing the point. The German's incredulity vanished; the girl, it appeared, had been telling the truth; to carry out the execution would be to make himself a target for revenge.

He made one stipulation—that in order to save him from punishment by the *Wehrmacht*, as from the *Maquis*, he should be taken away, and his personal protection assured. The girl agreed. So it was that hardly an hour before the time when they expected to die, Cammaerts and his two companions found their German captor at the door of their cell, key in hand, offering himself as their prisoner. Together they hurried to a car in which the girl was waiting, and drove to safety.

In this extraordinary young woman's response to the misfortune that had befallen the three British officers, we see the lucky mind in action: superior energy, manifesting itself in the confidence, presence of mind, and determination needed for so daring an enterprise; a high degree of empathic and creative imagination, giving the girl insight into the German's mind and enabling her to concoct a story both plausible and effective; and above all, a third primary ingredient, faith, which brought forth the courage needed to walk unflinchingly into danger, and accept what chance might bring, without losing hope. For only when faith is present is courage likely to be strong or long sustained. It is a point noted by many a military leader. Cromwell had to recruit his famed Ironsides from "such men as had the fear of God before them" in order to find a regiment that was fearless in the face of King Charles's cavalry.

Faith-founded courage reveals its luck-power, not only in crisis, but even more in the ordinary business of life. It is, for example, unmistakable that the finest leadership in the endless fight against tyranny, intolerance, and political cynicism comes from men to whom faith is a living part of life. Such men have the inner force required to challenge the shouting demagogue, to ask the searching question that gives pause to the unthinking mob, to risk unpopularity by telling a needed truth or denouncing a dangerous lie.

THE RELATION OF FAITH TO LUCK

The word "faith" is used here, not in the sense of conventional lip-service to a religious creed, but to signify the state of mind of those who are either wholly at one with their religion or who profoundly hold a philosophic belief from which flows an affirmation of life and a moral principle. So considered, faith does not end with church attendance, pious sentiments, and lofty aphorisms; it is the bedrock of a way of life. And it is bedrock unfortunately missing from many lives. Millions who complain of hard luck not only have failed to realize that their misfortunes grow out of insecure patterns of behavior; they are also unaware that their psychological insecurity stems largely from lack of faith in anything beyond the ego.

Many even take a kind of twisted pride in *not* having a faith. To them, an attitude of sneering disbelief in religion and contempt for philosophy seems somehow the stamp of a superior mind. Has not science negated religion, they demand? Are not philosophers always at loggerheads, unable to agree on anything? Then why waste time that can be better spent in the practical business of living? To people who hold this view professions of religious faith are taken to be the mark of superstition and ignorance, while philosophical speculation is a foolish game played by highbrows. The truth is, however, that the sophisticates who think in this way, far from being modern men, are woefully behind their age. They have not yet learned that in this century science, reversing its earlier position, has begun to come to the support of religion. Leading scientists—Einstein, Eddington, Millikan, Jeans, and others—have reached conclusions about the universe which, in many ways, resemble the mystical revelations at the core of the great religions. The truth is that not faith but the *fear* of faith is today the mark of ignorance. And unlucky indeed is the man who, unconditioned for religion, yet cannot find a solid foundation of faith in philosophy. True, philosophers disagree. But this is only to say that there is more than one route by which the mind can approach the peak of thought where men perceive the grandeur of universal law, and may be inspired by what Einstein has called "the cosmic religious sense."

Since this matter of faith bears strongly on our major

interest—the lucky life and how to attain it—we can afford to go further. It is safe to say that all attempts to satisfy the basic desire for faith with mundane substitutes are fundamentally unlucky. Sometimes men and women who have neither religion nor philosophy try to fill the void in their lives by pinning their faith on their children or on their work. In such cases, the chances of the years are all too likely to pull the props out from under them, leaving them wounded and bruised in a world that no longer has meaning for them. Love of one's children and respect for one's work can be strengthening influences. They cannot, however, take the psychological place of a profound identification between the self and some large religious or philosophic conception of good, which provides a moral basis for behavior.

Faith is an armor, it has been truly said, and men without it seldom realize, until misfortune overtakes them, the degree to which they stand naked and exposed to the wintry wind of adversity. For when we lack the steadying power of faith, the insecurity feelings latent in all of us tend to run away with our behavior. A psychologist who teaches at a university once made an informal study among his students of three negative traits, bragging, snobbishness, and secretiveness, all of which express insecurity. When he correlated the results with what he knew of the students' backgrounds and beliefs, there seemed to be an unmistakable link between the presence of these unlucky flaws of character and the absence of religious or philosophic faith.

Evidence from every side indicates that modern man's cynical inclination to disdain religion as a sign of stupidity and philosophy as a waste of time invites misfortune into countless lives. Psychiatrists know that the vast majority of their patients consist of those who have either lost or never held a firm faith that might have helped them bear up under the overload imposed on their minds by the mounting complexities of modern life. Whenever any intelligent individual looks at himself in relation to the world around him, a sense of frightful loneliness and peril is likely to grow in him and push him toward desperation unless he has a faith to cling to. Listen to unlucky Macbeth, crying out in reckless frenzy, "I would set my life on any chance, to mend it or be rid on't!" There we hear the cry of the man without faith, cut off from all the warm, human comforts, cold with despair, whose last hope is blind chance, and beyond that, nothing.

We can cite very specific reasons why luck is most likely to be found in the faith-directed way of life. Faith tends to develop in the individual certain attributes which go far to ensure successful responses to chance. Courage is one of these attributes. But no less important than courage in the luck-process are two other characteristics that are in good part the psychological offspring of faith: *integrity* and the *sense of proportion*. The significance of these qualities in the total fortunes of every man is so high as to deserve our concentrated attention.

INTEGRITY AS THE BASIS OF LUCK

To judge from all the evidence available, it is through the quality of integrity that faith chiefly affects our responses to chance. Not that we find integrity in every person who professes a religion or a philosophy. But wherever we do find a person of genuine integrity, there, almost by definition, we find a core of faith. Perhaps it is an unavowed faith, perhaps one of which the possessor is not even fully conscious. But the living force of integrity can grow only out of the seed of faith. The distinguishing characteristic of the integrated personality is that it puts moral principle above animal instinct and the claims of the ego. This exaltation of moral principle manifests a belief, however undeveloped, in universal law.

The luckiness of integrity, as a human attribute, lies largely in its power to keep our responses to chance free from weakening doubts of our sincerity and honesty

of purpose. The point can readily be seen in an actual
case—an episode in the life of Prime Minister Eamon de
Valera of Eire. In the year 1920 de Valera, then a young
leader of the movement for Irish independence, came to
America to enlist support. Not all Irish-Americans wel-
comed his presence. One powerful group in New York
felt a strong sense of rivalry with de Valera in reaching for
leadership of their common cause. So disturbed were they
by his vigorous activity that they decided to try to compel him to leave the country. To this end, a group of
seventy-five leading Irish-Americans, led by a well-known
judge, met at the Park Avenue Hotel in New York to de-
nounce de Valera, and to accuse him of "betraying the
cause" and "extravagant living."

Their idea was to discredit him by passing a resolution
which would then be given wide publicity, making any
subsequent efforts on his part useless. To get him out of
the way while they brought off this coup, they conceived
the idea of sending him a bogus invitation to address a
meeting in Chicago. De Valera accepted and was about to
catch a train westward, when someone came to him and
revealed the trap that had been set.

So far, chance had spoken; now de Valera's response was
at issue. A man lacking in integrity, or conscious of having
betrayed his trust, could not have acted with the serene

assurance that now characterized de Valera's movements. Appearing suddenly at the opposition meeting, he demanded the right to defend himself, was grudgingly granted permission to speak, and carried the crowd by sheer force of truth and personality. From that time on, his ascendancy over the independence movement was assured.

De Valera's luck in this instance illustrates the interplay of chance with the quality of integrity. It is, of course, obvious that the unexpected visit from the friend who warned him was an essential element in the chain of events; like other idealists, de Valera had established many luck-lines with men who shared his ideals. This warning, however, could not have brought him luck without the strength of response that integrity alone makes possible.

To bring one's full power to bear on any situation requires that the personality be integrated by belief in moral law—by faith. Unless the mind works as a whole to serve us, we cannot hope for much luck in life. Indeed, we may say that when we lose integrity, we lose an essential element in life itself. Throughout the entire universe, integrity is the key to existence. This is a point of utmost importance in the scheme of luck-development. We can never afford to forget that every failure in integrity literally takes away from life.

HOW FAILURE IN INTEGRITY
LEADS TO MISFORTUNE

To grasp fully the power of integrity to affect our lives and our fortunes, we do well to pause for a paragraph and lift our eyes to the universe as modern science sees it. Matter, science has shown us, consists of space made to look and feel substantial by fast-moving electrical charges. And here the scientist is confronted by a further remarkable fact. *Objects keep their shape.* Things we normally think of as "dead matter" actually put up a kind of passive resistance to disintegration. The table at which we write, the chair on which we sit, somehow hold on to the whirling electrons, to the positrons and the neutrons which compose their atoms and which are responsible for their appearance.

Even the loss of larger units is resisted. The rock grips its crystals with surprising tenacity in the face of the eroding forces of wind and stream. And not only the rock, but the earth, the solar system, the galaxy, cling to their star stuff, and keep their essential integrity of form in spite of forces working for their disintegration. As for living cells, they go so far as to perform work in order to prevent disintegration. Before its death, the living organism, in its urge to preserve integrity of form, instinctively perpetuates that form through its descendants.

The essence of life's struggle is this compulsion to

preserve structural integrity. And the struggle does not end with physical effort. The intricate and sensitive mind of which man is so proud can help him survive only when it works as an integrated unit. When the mind is split by a sense of moral failure, we are more weakened in the struggle of life than if we had lost a limb. The loss of integrity is a signpost on the road to self-destruction.

It is hardly surprising, then, to find that even the most well-meaning people are easily crushed by chance, if they lack a high standard of personal integrity. Let us analyze in this connection the story of a housewife living in a large suburban town near New York. She was one of millions of women without any intellectual or spiritual interest, content to drift from one day's problems to the next, concerned only with the physical aspects of living. One day on a commuters' train which was taking her to New York to shop, she struck up a pleasant acquaintance with another woman from the same town who, it turned out, was going to the same department store.

For a short period the housewife left her purse where her new acquaintance was standing, and moved out of sight. When she returned, she opened her bag and noticed that a twenty-dollar bill, which her husband had given her that morning, was not there. Immediately suspicious, she awaited an opportunity to open the purse of the other woman without being observed, and finally found one.

There, tucked into the corner, was a twenty-dollar bill; and filled with righteous indignation, the housewife pocketed it. The other woman returned, sensed a strain between them, remembered an engagement, and went away.

That night, when the housewife returned home, her husband called her attention to the twenty-dollar bill he had given her still lying on the table where she had left it. She was shattered. The tormenting realization that she was a thief, and fear of the loss of her reputation, caused her prolonged anxiety, and for years thereafter she was haunted by memory of the experience.

How much of this bad luck was due to chance, how much to unsound response? The lapse of memory—the opportunity to examine the other woman's purse surreptitiously—there spoke chance. Unsound judgment and defective self-respect led to a wrong appraisal of the chance, and the opening of the purse. Then—another chance—the presence of the second twenty-dollar bill. Now the crucial factor of response showed its power. Having discovered, as she thought, that her money had been stolen, what ought the housewife to have done?

For a person of integrity there were other possibilities. For example, upon the return of her new acquaintance, she might have exclaimed that she had lost the money—and wondered when and how. Observing the other woman's reaction, and seeing that it conveyed no consciousness of guilt, it would then have been natural to reconsider. Could the money have been lost elsewhere? Or left at home? These would have been normal questions for a person of integrity to ask herself—and to answer before assuming the guilt of another.

Beyond this, the woman of moral principle would have preferred to swallow the loss, however irritating at the moment, rather than violate her code. Experience teaches that minor monetary misfortunes soon pass from the memory, whereas a failure in integrity eats at the mind like an acid. This housewife's response was earmarked for misfortune. The lack of spiritual resources which led to her act of folly meant that she had no psychological defense against its unhappy aftermath. Without the firming influence of faith, without the respect for universal moral principle that is essential to integrity, she was an easy victim of casual mischance.

LUCK AND THE SENSE OF PROPORTION

Together with courage and integrity, a third lucky characteristic flows from faith—the wide-horizoned attitude of mind that we think of as a sense of proportion. This attitude expresses itself in the personality through humility and through humor. The man who sees his actual position in the universe, and who can endure the revelation of his personal unimportance, gains thereby enormous inner strength. Throughout life the sense of proportion links with chance to produce good luck and to mitigate misfortune.

The story of a young professor of science at a great university, a man of high ability and much personal charm, indicates the value of a sense of proportion in overcoming bad luck through sound response. Late one night, after attending a somewhat alcoholic party of youthful faculty members, he walked across the campus, found himself passing a girls' dormitory, and observed a lighted window, without a shade, where two girls could be seen undressing. In an uninhibited moment he yielded to the natural impulse to watch them—a sport, it may be added, in which many a male undergraduate had lightheartedly indulged.

In accepting this unfavorable chance the professor was unlucky. Another chance brought a night watchman to the spot at that very instant, and he took the professor into custody as a Peeping Tom. The resulting punishment seemed altogether disproportionate to the triviality of the offense. Not only was he fired from the university, but someone told the press, so that newspaper headlines blared out his disgrace; and other faculty members smugly predicted that his career as a scientist and teacher was finished.

This man had no formal religious faith to sustain him in the wreck of his career. He did, however, have a scientist's perception of the awesomeness of the universe in which men act out their lives. He believed that the universal laws revealed by science bespoke an unknowable purpose in existence and that the observed facts of the cosmos obliged the individual to recognize his personal insignificance and to accept what came to him with dignity and humility.

Instead of trying to excuse himself for his act of folly, instead of indulging in despair or self-pity, he went to another part of the country. There he visited a college dean whom he knew and explained with candor and humor precisely what had happened. For a while to come, he was aware, no faculty would wish to risk the embarrassment of his presence on it; he would have to expiate his crime; but perhaps he might quietly work in the college laboratories as a research-fellow, and so carry on his chosen work? The dean agreed, and so without complaint the young man began his career over again on the lowest rung of the academic ladder. A few years later, when time had wiped the episode out of memory, his exceptional abilities made themselves so widely felt that he was rapidly elevated to high status on the college faculty, and became one of the most useful and respected members of his profession. A sense of proportion, deriving from his philosophical faith, had helped him to sustain a heavy blow from chance—and by wise response, to emerge as a whole and happy man.

THE UNLUCKINESS OF ENVY

This same quality, the sense of proportion derived from religion or philosophy, has a further bearing on our fortunes through its power in combating envy, among the unluckiest of human characteristics. Now it is obvious enough that everyone, including the man of faith, feels envy frequently in his life. Competitive beings that we are, we can hardly be expected to cheer at the success of our rivals for life's stakes. Most of us are like the playwright who remarked, only half in jest, that every time he read that another man's play was a hit his hair turned green. But if envy is quickly controlled by a sense of proportion, it does little harm. In fact, a feeling of envy may be transformed into healthy admiration and spur men to make more of their abilities. The great polar explorer Amundsen said that when he heard that Commodore Peary had reached the North Pole, his first thought was, "Then I shall visit both Poles." And he did.

The danger to luck arises when envy is unchecked and becomes a permanent state of mind, for then it stands between us and successful responses to chance. Whatever we may tell ourselves, it is not hard luck that makes us envious so much as envy that makes us unlucky. Grudging contemplation of the good lives of others lays us open to prompt reprisals by fortune. In a typical case, a young business executive by chance heard a rumor that one of his co-workers was about to be promoted to a position higher than his own. Lacking a sense of proportion, and regarding himself as the center of the universe, he was an easy victim for bad luck.

Envy went to work, and produced a characteristic response. He had heard some fact slightly discreditable to his rival. Now he made an opportunity, apparently accidental, to talk with the president of his company and, in the course of the conversation, to let this derogatory fact fall. The president listened, said nothing, and withheld the promotion from the unwitting victim. But at the same time—and this the envious man never knew—he had talked himself out of a promotion for which he had been slated. The reason given by the president in an executive meeting was that this man "seemed not to have much loyalty to his fellow workers"—an accurate diagnosis, since loyalty and unchecked envy cannot live together.

Nor do we add much to our luck-potential by pretending not to be envious when we are. Some men of envious disposition have, like Iago, learned to dissimulate their feelings, and to wear a mask of sweet friendship toward the more successful, but they seldom are able to maintain the deception. Usually there are several unfailing marks of the envious man. A seething broil of insecurity feelings, he tends to be a boaster and a braggart, if sometimes a subtle one. He is deficient in humor. Consumed by envy, he likes to arouse it in others, parading any temporary superiority over his acquaintances and playing on their frustrations by letting them see that he has what they want. Above all, unhappiness looks out of his face, reflecting the truth that Chaucer wrote long ago, "There standeth Envie and holdeth the hot iron on the heart of a man." It is typical of the envious that while they wish misfortune to others, and inflict it when they can with impunity, they are themselves made miserable by their feelings. As Bertrand Russell says, "Instead of deriving pleasure from what he has, he (the envious man) derives pain from what others have."

We cannot do much to protect ourselves against the envy of others, but we can at least safeguard our luck against the temptation to make envious responses to the chances that we ourselves meet. The strength which comes to men when they have faith in something beyond the self—the sense of proportion which gives them perspective on their lives—these are the best weapons against the unlucky curse of enviousness. The man with a sense of proportion may feel envy now and then, but he beats it down by the knowledge that it is unworthy of him, and refuses to let it dictate his behavior.

THE LUCKY ROAD TO FAITH

The envy-resisting sense of proportion—rooted integrity—sustained courage—those are stars of the first magnitude in luck's constellation; and faith is their parent-quality. The need of effort to develop these attributes is too plain to need much discussion. What must be stressed is the point that any such effort, if it is to succeed, must follow the spiritual and intellectual route toward faith.

Although faith cannot be acquired merely by wishing for it, a strong urge to believe in something beyond the self is the foundation from which we reach upward toward conviction. Persons who feel this urge, regardless of the circumstances of their lives, are lucky if they yield to it. Too often we shrug away our instinctive hunger for faith, without realizing its great bearing on our ultimate direction. It is important for every faith-starved person to recognize that there are specific steps that he can take to fill the unlucky void of non-faith in his personality. Those steps are obvious enough. We can, for example, talk with men of faith who out of their experience and wisdom may suggest the path best graded to our climbing-power. We

can read books at the highest level of thought at which
we are capable, which tell of the efforts of others to achieve
faith. We can take an occasional hour to go off by ourselves, sit on a hilltop or a friendly chair, and try to con-
template without fear or hate the universe we live in and
our relation to it. At the very least, this effort of solitude
carries refreshment to the jaded mind. When it becomes
a discipline, aimed at enlarging our grasp of universal law,
it can sometimes bring one very close to faith. Those who
lack a conclusive spiritual revelation, and yet wish to understand the nature of religion and philosophy, can often
find in these ways insights so deep as to tap the reserves
of psychic strength which we need in order to accept life
as it is, and love it.

It would, of course, be ridiculous to say, "I wish to be
lucky; therefore I shall get me a faith." The urge to faith,
if it is to be a serviceable springboard to the lucky life,
must arise from an intuitive perception of a mystery in
existence, from the felt need of a larger view of the universe than we can find in the prison of the ego. Nor should
the seeker for faith assume that it will be easy to achieve
his goal. Currently there is a widespread demand for faith-
without-tears; people beset by care often think that, if
they espouse an accepted religion or psychological doc-
trine, they can leap at one bound to the peace of mind for

which holy men and thinkers throughout history have groped through arduous and painful years. Not faith, but an easy escape from reality is their goal; they want to rid themselves of their troubles without ever coming to grips with the real problems of their existence. An avowal of faith, it seems to them, ought to keep them free of misfortune; and if it does not, they feel let down. When they fail, as they must, to find the overnight panacea that they seek, they drop their new creed as easily as they adopted it and try another, reverting at last to hopeless materialism.

The lucky life requires faith, not to shut out suffering, but to help in the acceptance of pain, to strengthen responses to misfortune, and to develop the personality to its full limits. Faith is an armor, true, but it is an "armor of light." As Dante told us, the serene state of faith, Paradise, is approached through a purgatory in which men learn enlightenment—learn to face reality, to think hard, to feel deeply, to accept pain and to look beyond it. It is in this sense that the strengthening or acquisition of faith represents the capstone of our personal development.

Together with high energy and strong imagination, faith makes for sound responses to the chances of the world. If, to effective response, we add the power to attract favorable chances, and to recognize them in time, we have the full potential of the lucky life. Few, of course, are completely equipped by nature for luck. Most of us must try, by conscious effort, to raise our luck-potential by strengthening our positive attributes and by guarding against insecure patterns of behavior. But the road to better luck is well-marked, the goal clearly within view; all that is needed now to begin the ascent is *the will to be lucky.*

CONCLUSION:
THE WILL TO BE LUCKY

*"Determine on some course, More than
a wild exposure to each chance."*

SHAKESPEARE

As a comet on its erratic path through the heavens is constantly bombarded by the meteors of space, so the energetic bundle of desire that is man moves among the external chances of his world, touched on every side by the unexpected. Each chance, as it strikes into his life, has its influence, altering the life-course of the individual, slightly or greatly, for better or for worse. Man, however, is a comet with consciousness. Possessing some freedom of choice, he can steer away from this chance, accept and be guided by that one; he can, in other words, influence his own direction in life, the extent of his fulfillments, his luck.

This conscious steering of our actions, which is the peculiar privilege of man, is a skill that must be learned. The successful steersman in life, the lucky man, requires a degree of mastery of the difficult arts of behavior and self-expression. Certain specific qualities of character and personality need to be developed in us before we can find a lucky way through life. These qualities are, so to speak, our certificates of stock in Fortune and Company, that bountiful corporation which keeps on declaring extra dividends of happiness and achievement for its limited membership. When we sometimes say, perhaps with a touch of envy, that So-and-so is "naturally lucky," we may intend to convey that he has been unduly favored by chance. Actually, the phrase tells the aware that the chances of inheritance and conditioning, by their mysterious alchemy, have given So-and-so a personality which moves in harmony with chance—a personality which instinctively knows how to attract, recognize, and respond to favorable chances.

Even if we are not ourselves naturally lucky, we can at least bring more luck into our lives than we have had. The extent to which we make ourselves luckier is likely to be directly proportional to the force of our will to be lucky. When that will is strong, when men have a keen sense of their own responsibility for their fortunes in life, they can influence their luck far more than they usually dare to dream.

The chances of life, from which luck flows, serve as a kind of cosmic membership committee, constantly testing our readiness for admittance to the exclusive lodge of the lucky. When our personality undergoes a constructive change, chance soon finds it out, as some unexpected event taps the new source of strength within us. All that chance demands of us is an effort to become luckier than we are. If we make that effort, chance will do the rest. *The will to be lucky* is the crux of our internal development, the channel through which we can realize our full potentialities as lucky human beings.

Everyone feels this—and yet many people who think that they are willing to make the requisite effort to be lucky actually are deluding themselves. It seems to them that because they have resolved to do something, they have actually begun to do it. But as everyone who has ever forgotten a New Year's resolution knows, a large psychological gap exists between resolve and effort, especially sustained effort. Even when the importance of the effort to our fortunes is recognized, the will often dissipates itself in a day, or an hour.

For this prevailing tendency of good resolve to come to nothing, there are three common reasons. One reason is simply that the person who makes the resolution does not fully understand what he is trying to do. The second reason is lack of a specific plan of action for carrying out the intention. And finally, we have the fact that most people who make such resolutions in their enthusiasm usually try to do too much at one time. It is fitting here to examine these three problems and to see how, in the interests of luck-development, we can best overcome them.

WHAT ARE WE TRYING TO DO?

To make our behavior luckier, however slightly, is a task which requires insight. The wish may be father to the act, but we cannot forget that most of our behavior is born out of habit. It is through our habitual patterns of action that we express our personality traits. However ardently we may wish to develop some aspect of the personality, we cannot go far unless we are able to modify old patterns of behavior.

It is our actions that nourish our personalities. A quality that is not expressed in action tends to wither away. It is when we modify or replace an undesirable pattern of behavior with a luckier one that we bring our luck-charged attributes of personality into freer play, and make it easier for chance to help us fulfill our desires.

Suppose, for example, that we are conscious of a deficiency in zest. We say to ourselves, "From now on, I shall be more zestful." Immediately, the problem arises: how, specifically, shall we express this resolve? It is not enough to say that we must really talk to more people or read more good books. This intention immediately comes into conflict with our established ways of using our time.

Let us say that, suffering from shyness, we like to eat solitary lunches while we flip through a picture magazine; and that we are accustomed to spend our evenings, regularly, looking at television. These escapist patterns of behavior may be negative, they may represent the unlucky path of least resistance in our lives, but *they are habits*. One cannot yank an entrenched habit out of oneself like a tooth. Its roots often go deep into our psychic life. *To change a habit requires first that we dislike it*. We must understand its psychological significance, and resent it with sufficient intensity of feeling so that we generate the energy and determination necessary to replace it. Not until we have this strong feeling can we break with the patterns of behavior which block our way to the development of lucky attributes.

An actual case helps to make the point. It is the story of a business executive who frequently had conferences in the afternoon. Habitually a heavy eater, he was observed, just before one important meeting, sitting long at the luncheon table and stuffing himself. Inevitably, his digestion in the ensuing hour demanded energy needed by his brain, with the result that he was lethargic and slow-witted in the conference, made an unfavorable impression, and did his career serious harm. Now he was an intelligent man; he knew that he habitually consumed too much food for his needs; he knew the importance of alertness in his business. Often he had resolved to eat less, to diet, to "watch his figure." Yet when it came to the test, he "forgot" all this, and ate to excess, at the worst possible time for his luck.

We may say that he lacked the will to break his unlucky pattern of behavior. But the real reason goes much deeper. What he really lacked was *understanding of what he was trying to do*—of the psychological reason for his bad habit.

That reason, in his case, is not hard to find. Today psychologists recognize that the excessive consumption of food (like that of alcohol and tobacco) touches infantile desires buried deep in our nervous systems for the use of our lips to allay feelings of insecurity. As the infant ceases to cry when he finds his mother's breast, as the baby gets pleasure from sucking its thumb, so we often feel soothed by the mere action of taking food in through our lips. Studies by medical groups have shown that most over-weight people tend to eat more when they are worried and anxious than at other times. So, too, with the chain-smoker and chronic alcoholic. The desire to use the lips and dull the consciousness in order to escape from anxiety may drive them to the second package of cigarettes, or to the third double whiskey, as it drives the fat man to the refrigerator for the midnight snack.

To modify habits with such strong roots, *we must feel active resentment of the insecurity feelings that push us into inferior patterns of behavior.* For it is these feelings that prevent us from developing luckier personalities. When we arrive at understanding of what we are trying to do, and when that understanding gives rise to the requisite strength of feeling, then, and only then, the will to be lucky can be fully effective. The businessman whose case is described above could not develop alertness until he recognized that his habit of overeating revealed an inner sense of insecurity. Then a feeling of dissatisfaction with himself at last generated the active force needed for the lucky effort of self-discipline.

THE LINE OF ACTION

That effort consisted of modifying his mealtime pattern of behavior. In his case, it was plain that the point at which a hearty meal turned into excess was the dessert, for he was inordinately fond of rich desserts. What he needed was a departure in his eating habits that would help him to resist this temptation. The change he hit upon was simple but effective. He compelled himself, immediately after the main course, to rise from the table and occupy himself with other matters. Simple though this may sound, it was not an easy achievement; but sustained over a period of weeks, it became a habit, replacing the old habit of the dessert. This single, successful effort of the will to be lucky had far-reaching consequences. It showed itself not only in this man's increased alertness, but in his health, his state of mind, and his total fortunes thereafter.

It may be asked: How can a new pattern of behavior take root and survive while the sense of insecurity still persists? Even if it does survive, will not the insecurity feelings merely seek another, equally destructive outlet in our behavior? Here we come to a fact of utmost importance in giving expression to our will to be lucky. *We make ourselves more secure in spirit when we habitually act as if we are secure.* There is a reciprocal relation between our behavior and our psychic life. As the sense of security induces strong patterns of behavior, so the strong pattern of behavior builds up the inner sense of security.

Any effort we make, however slight, to prevent the dictation of our behavior by insecurity feelings is a step toward luckiness. Our first need in striving for better luck is to change or strengthen some inferior pattern of behavior. When we decide on this effort, it is important to translate it promptly into a specific line of action. If our will to be lucky is not to be wasted, we need to have clearly in mind *a constructive substitute* for the behavior pattern that we propose to change.

Consider, for example, the case of a man who became conscious of the fact that he often boasted, and that his boasting was unlucky for him since it resulted in negatively charged luck-lines. He determined to stop boasting. Soon thereafter he met an acquaintance, felt a desire to impress him by talking of his business successes, and managed to suppress the words.

So far, so good. Feeling virtuous, he thought he was on his way to overcoming his unlucky habit. Actually, he had not even made a dent in it. The desire to allay his insecurity feelings by arousing the envy of another was still in him. In a short time, he realized that he was still boasting.

He was, however, intelligent enough to perceive that the lax egoism which aroused contempt in men whose good opinion he valued could only be held in check if he practiced a different approach in his chance contacts with others. His need was for a *constructive substitute* for the habit of boasting, and in time he managed to develop one. The specific technique which he employed was the asking of questions. Instead of saying, "I've just had my pay raised again!" to a poor devil who he knew could not make ends meet, he would, from the first moment of meeting, seek for questions that he might ask—even if no more than "How do you manage to keep so fit?" or "Where did you go on your vacation?" The essential thing was to shift the theme of his conversation away from his own vanity and to the interests of the other person.

In so doing, he was not only strengthening his invitation to luck but actually making himself a more secure personality. Each time that he succeeded in conquering his egotistical impulses, he was in effect assuring himself that he did not need to boast—that he did not depend on the paltry ego-gratification the boast gave him. In this way, he acted to transform himself into a man of increased force of character, and with far greater power to attract favorable chances.

FOCUS YOUR EFFORT SHARPLY

Once we understand the problem, once we have developed a specific line of action and have found constructive substitutes for unlucky behavior patterns, we are well on the way to a higher luck-potential. However, we still need to guard against another common cause of failure to get results from the will to be lucky. Often people try to do too much at once—to "make themselves over." It is a hopeless enterprise. The same man may be shy, ungenerous, lacking in confidence, hungry for flattery, and envious; he may suffer from indigestion, be cynical about religion, and mean to his wife. He may even recognize these faults in himself, but it is a virtual certainty that if he tries to correct all of them at once, he will only be wasting his time.

A single modest improvement at a time is the goal—and it is often enough to produce far-reaching consequences in one's fortunes. We have examined, in this book, the importance to our luck of a number of characteristics which have an especially close relationship to the workings of chance: zest and generosity, with their power to attract luck into our lives; alertness, self-knowledge, judgment, self-respect, and intuition—all of high value in the recognition of favorable chances; and qualities of especial significance in our responses to chance—energy, with its bearing on presence of mind, confidence, and determination—imagination—and the courage, sense of proportion, and integrity that grow out of faith. We make far greater progress by concentrating our initial effort on a single one of these qualities that lies within easy reach than by trying to become something that we are not capable of being.

As an example, Arnold Bennett, a man who believed strongly in self-improvement and practiced what he preached, was shy and envious and something of a snob all his life, and knew it. His answer to his problem was to direct his efforts largely to the systematic use of his energy in work, reading, and play. This was enough to bring him exceptional luck at crucial points in his career. If he had tried instead to be a saint, he probably would have wound up neither saint nor success.

Like Bennett, we are well-advised to pick for a beginning in luck-development a promising characteristic which is merely underdeveloped rather than one in which we are gravely deficient. Often a good guide will be found in one's own interests. Our effort is likely to be far more productive of lucky results if it is directed to the development of a quality that excites our imagination and comes close to our desires than if we pour energy into activity that bores us, even if we regard it as worthy.

We must avoid, too, muddling our minds with a confusion of "do's" and "don'ts." The more sharply focused our effort is, the more likely it is to yield prompt results in better luck. Take the case of a man who realizes that frequent boredom is damaging his luck—causing him, in his eagerness for new sensations, to accept unfavorable chances. If he tries to do twenty things to correct this condition, he will plunge into a whirl of meaningless activity that in the end can only leave him more jaded and bored than ever. His need is to find a specific pursuit that will fill the gap in his life and hold his interest. At the moment when he selects a line of action and makes the first move that breaks with the deadening routines of his life—at the moment when, in pursuit of fresh activity, he puts on his hat, picks up a telephone, or sits down to write a letter—that is when he opens the door for a constructive change in his fortunes.

In opening that door, we do well to swing it confidently and boldly. Whenever an unlucky habit needs to be broken, whether of diet or speech or behavior, we make headway when we symbolize the change to ourselves at once by a forthright, strong action at the very beginning. If we cannot be strong at the beginning of the effort, we are hardly likely to be able to sustain it. The sooner and the more vigorously we begin to establish the new line of action, the sooner our luck will improve, as chance plays upon the strengthened personality.

By doing a few relatively simple things over a period of a few months, men can often develop the lucky side of their personalities to an extent that seems miraculous. With a normal play of chance, an increase in one's potential luckiness does not take long to show itself in better luck and greater happiness.

Vast and ungovernable is the power of chance; and yet,

as we have seen, its influence on our luck is profoundly shaped by our own actions. The presence of this book in your hand is itself a chance, and your response to it may go far to affect your fortune to come.

And now—good luck!

ABOUT THE AUTHOR

A. H. Z. Carr (1902–1971) was a consulting economist for several major corporations, an economic adviser to the Roosevelt presidency, and a consultant to the Truman presidency. Carr authored several books, and his writing appeared in *Harper's*, *The Saturday Evening Post*, and *Reader's Digest*.

If you enjoyed this book, visit

www.tarcherbooks.com

and sign up for Tarcher's e-newsletter to receive
special offers, giveaway promotions, and
information on hot upcoming releases.

TARCHER
PENGUIN

Great Lives Begin with Great Ideas

Connect with the Tarcher Community

. . .

Stay in touch with favorite authors!
Enter weekly contests!
Read exclusive excerpts!
Voice your opinions!

Follow us

 Tarcher Books

 @TarcherBooks

If you would like to place a bulk order
of this book, call 1-800-847-5515.